The Place B

A True and Beautiful Near-Death Experience

Figure 1 - Sunrise over Callahan's Beach, Ft Salonga, Long Island

By Katherine Plant and Stephen Weber

First Edition published by Between Here and There, LLC – Fort Salonga, NY

Proofread by Angela Blanchet and Sean Reilly
Book cover and logo design by Nada Orlic and Rachel Titone.
All photographs are by Katherine Plant and Stephen Weber unless otherwise noted.

www.BetweenHereAndThere.org – info@BetweenHereAndThere.org

Life is good and people are good
even when sad things happen.

Table of Contents

Dedication

This book is dedicated to Nancy Hume, a beautiful 85-year old yogi that touched our hearts and souls immensely during our spiritual journey together. Born in 1934, Nancy was one of the pioneers of the yoga scene back when yoga was not as cool as it is today and was mostly the pastime of "peace-nicks" and "hippies." We met Nancy at our first yoga class at Kundalini Yoga of Long Island in Northport, New York. With a bright smile, sparkling eyes, and a radiant glow, she welcomed us to the practice with an open heart and an open soul. The connection was instant, and we felt like we knew Nancy forever.

Figure 2 -Nancy Hume at Sat Nam Fest 2019, Photograph by Katie Clark

It was immediately apparent that Nancy was in our soul group, which is the group of souls with whom you come to Earth for soul growth and enlightenment. Everyone has a soul group, which is not necessarily the members of their biological family, but those who have profoundly assisted them most in this lifetime and possibly others.

Nancy became our mentor, and an example of how to live life spiritually, with her infinite wisdom and photographic memory of all things spiritual. She also became our example of how to live life physically. Defying nature and the limitation of aging, Nancy attends daily yoga classes and looks "textbook" while performing yoga poses. She can hold those poses for as long as required, which is sometimes for an excruciatingly long amount of time. Another quality of Nancy's that is so astonishing is her positivity.

The joy and light with which this woman lives life is an example for all beings. She loves all people and judges no one. Nancy is equally passionate about all living things, spiritual masters, and mother Earth. Most significant of all, however, is that Nancy is the reason why this book was written. She is our inspiration. That is why we had to devote this book to Nancy. It is because of our love for her that this story is now in print – an eternal love and one that we share in this lifetime and will definitely share in more lifetimes to come.

Foreword

Being a "live and let live" kind of guy and not really thinking much about my life purpose or what happened after life on Earth, I lived each day based on physical existence and not based on any spiritual matters whatsoever. The topic of life after death was not one that crossed my mind often, and I will honestly say that it could have been because it is a terrifying topic. If you are not a spiritual person, pondering the afterlife could lead to anxiety and stress and the possible realization that maybe there is nothing after this existence. Avoiding the topic made life easier and more carefree. Partying and living in the ego are a beautiful escapism from reality, although I have since learned otherwise. My first real reason to ponder the afterlife was the result of my friendship with Gil (Pinky) Harris.

Gil was a "raconteur," which is what the French define as someone who is skilled at telling stories filled with both humorous anecdotes and words of wisdom. After his retirement, Gil liked to sit on a bench at the Kings Park Psychiatric Center, the local state mental hospital which was turned into a state park after being shuttered in 1996.

The Kings Park Psychiatric Center was not only a self-sustaining mental health hospital, complete with farming facilities, its own railroad, and a power plant, but it was also a beautiful 800-acre waterfront property that was a popular visiting place for curiosity seekers as well as prior staff and patients. During my daily hikes, I would walk through the property and often stop and sit with Gil to listen to his tales of times past.

Gil served in the Navy aboard a destroyer during the Cuban Missile Crisis. After his dad's passing, he came to Kings Park from North Carolina to work at the psychiatric hospital where his dad had worked. He even obtained his dad's old position as a storeroom worker. Gil assured the storehouse manager that he would work just as hard as his dad. The manager replied, "Just half as much would be fine, your dad was that good of a man."

Gil was a very kind gentleman who always looked at the brighter side of situations, and his humanity was demonstrated with every word. Due to his past in the U.S. Navy and his tenure of 16 years of employment at the Kings Park Psychiatric Center, Gil had lots of stories to tell and lots of wisdom to impart. To add more fodder to his story-telling cannon, Gil even worked as a bartender at The Round Table, a local bar and grill on the psychiatric center property, which was frequented by both the hospital patients with day passes and the staff.

Sometimes my friends and I would go to The Round Table and play a game, "guess who is patient and who is staff," and fifty percent of the time we were wrong. Gil knew who was who, so he enjoyed a good chuckle from our guesses. He knew everyone, and he knew everything about everyone. It was always a pleasure to hear Gil tell his grand tales, with his twinkling eyes and infectious grin.

I got so used to seeing Gil that when he stopped coming to his bench, after several days of his absence, I decided to give him a call. I was relieved when he answered right away and assured me that all was okay. He had accepted a part-time job working for an elderly lady for whom his wife, Maddalen, was a cook. He said that he was going to do odd jobs around her house and do her shopping. Gil had been retired for quite some time, and as much as I enjoyed our talks, he needed something more than that park bench. He assured me that it was only a few hours a day, and that when he got used to things, he would still have some time to chat with me.

Figure 3 - King Pedlar, Gil Harris, and Steve, Kings Park State Psychiatric Center

Several weeks went by and Gil had not returned to the bench. So, once again I gave him a call and asked him how he was doing. Gil said that the job was going well, although it did take a bit more time than he had previously anticipated. The elderly lady was almost blind now, and he would sit with her for several hours a day just to talk. This basically meant that he had a new audience for his stories. Gil said that she also liked to play cards, so he bought a large-print deck of cards, which she was able to decipher, so he could play cards with her. Gil told me that he lost most of the card games, with a humorous tone in his voice.

We laughed a bit, and I mentioned that while I did miss him, it was a beautiful thing that he was doing, and that I was sure that the extra money must be helpful. He quickly interrupted and said that he did not charge her any extra money for talking with her or playing cards. He just did not think it was right. He enjoyed spending time with her, and she had no one else to talk to. Most of her family and friends were long gone, so he and Maddalen were all she had. That was typical Gil.

Several weeks later, I noticed that Gil was back on his bench. I was thrilled to see him and told him so. He gave me a half smile, and I knew right away that something was troubling him. I asked what was wrong and if it was something that he would like to share with me. Gil said that over the past few weeks, the elderly lady's health began to deteriorate quite rapidly. She was basically bedridden. Gil would bring food to her each evening on a tray, sit with her, and help her feed herself. They still talked for hours, but, by now, she had trouble sitting up and could barely see at all. A depression began to invade her otherwise bright spirit. Gil had been around many people in their final days, so it was not that he was fearful of her passing. It was simply that he wanted her to be at peace and, right now, she was very far from that.

One evening, he brought food up to her room, and saw the elderly lady sitting up in her bed, frightened, with tears streaming down her cheeks. Gil quickly put the tray down, sat beside her, held her hand, and asked what was wrong. She said that she was at the bus stop, and she was frightened. There were a lot of strangers there, and she did not know what was going on. Without missing a beat, Gil stroked her forearm and asked, "Are they nice people?" She paused for a moment and mannered as if she was looking around, and then she replied that they were nice people, kind people, and beautiful people. "So, you have nothing to fear," Gil replied. She smiled and laid back down and allowed Gil to feed her as if nothing at all had just happened.

The next day, Gil brought food to the elderly lady in bed. He was quite surprised to see her once again sitting up, but this time she was smiling and rocking back and forth, just like Stevie Wonder or Ray Charles did when they played their pianos back in the olden days. Gil asked, "Are you at the bus stop?" and the lady replied that she was and that there were more nice people there that day.

Gil said this went on for several days. Then one evening, when Gil brought the elderly lady dinner, he noticed that she was sitting up in bed, smiling gently, and in a beautiful and peaceful state. When Gil asked if she was still at the bus stop, she replied that she was, but that the bus was coming and that she will be leaving soon to go on a trip. Gil asked where she was going, and she said that she did not know, but that she did know that it was a beautiful place. Then Gil asked if he could go with her. The lady responded, "No, the bus is full now, but I will tell the bus driver about how kind you and Maddalen have been to me, and I am sure he will save a seat for both of you when you are ready."

Early the next morning Gil received "the call." The elderly lady had passed during the previous night. Gil said that he was sad to see her go, but that he has seen enough to learn that there is a place beyond which we know, and with his characteristically Gil grin, he went on to say that now he knows that he has a seat saved on the bus. Not too long ago,

Gil took the bus ride to that beautiful place. I am sure that he is awaiting the arrival of his precious Maddalen after her work here on Earth is complete, and I am sure he is playing cards with the old lady again. Maybe she lets him win occasionally now.

At Gil's funeral, I spoke with his wife Maddalen. She was obviously grieving her soulmate's absence, but, looking back at what she and Gil learned from the old lady's ride on the bus, she was comforted by the affirmation of everlasting life, the continuation of the soul, and that she will see them again.

With this book, we hope to help those who are grieving a loss or who are just seeking answers to what, if anything at all, comes after this life. Within these pages you will learn that life is eternal, that life is beautiful, and that life is perfect just the way it is.

Chapter 1: The Accident

"On a cycle, the frame is gone. You're completely in contact with it all. You're in the scene, not just watching it anymore, and the sense of presence is overwhelming."

–Robert M. Pirsig, *The Zen of Motorcycle Maintenance*

The day had a beautiful calmness to it. It was April, and the trees were newly budding, the birds were singing, and the open road was calling me. I had just purchased a new Harley Davidson motorcycle, and I wanted to take a drive out east with my then-wife. That is how we kept the peace, even though we were nearing the end of our relationship. It was clear for many years already that we would inevitably go our separate ways. In fact, not only was it apparent to us, it was apparent to everyone around us.

We raised two beautiful children together, and she was a wonderful person, but we just grew apart over the years. The plan was to "play nice," and keep it together until the kids were in college. So, one of the things we liked to do, in an attempt to enjoy some time together, was to ride my motorcycle out to Eastern Long Island to dine at our favorite barbeque place for lunch. Since I had my brand-new Harley, I was anticipating an especially fun outing, and I was really looking forward to the long ride.

You can say that I was a biker, as I might have resembled one a little bit, but the truth is that I was really just a "motorcycle enthusiast" that just so happened to look like an "outlaw biker," complete with tattoos, long hair, and a leather jacket. It all began when I was 12 years old. I grew up in a town on Long Island called Kings Park, and my first job was delivering newspapers. Most of the kids with paper routes had bicycles, but I wanted to deliver my papers in style, on a cool-as-hell dirt bike. I had to start with my bicycle, but when I had saved up enough money, despite the opposition from my father, I bought my first dirt bike. It was a most joyous moment. I absolutely loved the money I earned from my paper route, but, most of all, I absolutely loved the fact that I had a cool-as-hell dirt bike because Kings Park has miles and miles of trails on which I could do a more serious type of riding.

Figure 4 - Steve circa 1974

Those days taught me a lot about bike handling, so by the time I was old enough to get a real motorcycle, riding came very easy to me. Over the years, I have traveled all over the United States by bike, to places such as California, Florida, North Dakota, Wisconsin, Illinois, and more. I was quite a confident rider, and even after a few minor accidents, I always got back up on the bike. Nothing stirred fear in me when it came to riding my motorcycle. Those trips were some of the fondest memories of my life. I just loved the travel, the freedom, and the outdoors. Most of all, I just loved those Harley Davidsons. I owned many Harley Davidsons over the years. One thing the Harley was known for was its loud roar. When I rode my Harley, people knew I was coming.

During those ego-driven years, I loved to "announce my presence with authority," with a loud blast of "the pipes." One year, my neighbors actually held a meeting to discuss the loudness of my bike, the speed at which I drove, and my "irregular" hours. They elected representatives to discuss the issues with me. There was really nothing I could do about it other than to bring my guitar and some drinks to the meeting and make friends with them. Afterwards, they tended to ignore my audial disturbances... most of the time.

Figure 5 - Steve on his Harley Davidson Road King, Canal Street, NYC

This new Harley Davidson, which I had just purchased, was quite different than any other I ever had. To the pleasure of my neighbors, it was actually very quiet. It was beautiful. It boasted a high-tech GPS system and a spectacular sound system. It was so comfortable that I felt like I was riding a couch down the street. I found out about this particular bike when I was visiting my mom in Florida and rented the same model Harley. It was such an awesome experience that when I got home, I immediately sold my old Harley and bought this new quiet and comfortable one.

This Harley was only a few days old, so when we boarded it to go out to the barbeque place, I was in my glory. After a beautiful and comfortable drive, accompanied by some Creed playing on the awesome sound system, we enjoyed our lunch and left the restaurant at about 4:00 p.m. Unfortunately, we were greeted by several miles of bumper-to-bumper traffic. It appeared there was some kind of roadwork being done, which was a bit odd for a Sunday, so there must have been an emergency road repair ahead.

We sat in this traffic for about a half hour, moving a foot or so every now and then. There was a right turn up in the distance, and several cars had passed us driving on the right shoulder of the road to make that right turn, presumably to avoid waiting in traffic any longer. This new Harley was quite a heavy bike. So, after witnessing several people make successful right turns, I decided to try and do the same so that I would not have to hold the bike up any longer.

I pulled into the right shoulder, and just as I approached the right turn, a car in the marked lane made room for an oncoming SUV that was driving in the opposite direction, so that he could make a left turn onto the same street that I was approaching. As soon as I entered the intersection, the truck "t-boned" into my bike, since neither of us were able to see each other. Further, with the quietness of the new bike, my presence was not as obvious as it would have been with my old Harley. Right then, I was thrown from my bike, and the lights went out.

When I came to, I was lying face up on the roadway, and an emergency worker was administering first aid to me. I had the feeling that quite a bit of time had passed since being hit, and my instinct was that I had better get up and shake this off. That is what I learned from my dirt bike days, and right or wrong, our mantra was "get up or stay down." Over the stern objections of the medical professionals, I attempted just that - to get up.

As soon as I moved, I felt a stabbing pain in my left hip, a pain that I had never felt before. My leg felt like it was disconnected from my hip, and I could feel the sharp edges of the bone fragments stuck like needles into my flesh. I knew immediately that there was no way I was getting up and that this day was not going to be like any other day I had ever experienced before. I knew my life would change forever. I laid back down on the road and everything faded to black again.

My next recollection was that I was rising up through the clouds and was able to look down at the accident scene. It seemed odd to me, since in my mind, I had just been back down on the pavement and writhing in pain. Yet I was now just floating up through the clouds without feeling anything. I could see my beautiful brand-new Harley in pieces laying on the ground. I could see the truck with which I had collided. There were also cars lined up for miles, and I was sure they were frustrated that they were stuck in even worse traffic now.

The higher I went, the smaller and less significant everything became. Nothing seemed to matter anymore. I was slipping into a peaceful state, and in my own way, I accepted the new reality that I was dying. I was ready to surrender to the experience. Then, suddenly, something unexpected happened. Rather than rising through the clouds to go to Heaven, I was actually descending the clouds and approaching the ground. I noticed a very big building with a large circle on the pavement, and I recognized where I was. I was at Stony Brook University Hospital. I was in a helicopter, and we were landing on the bullseye-painted helipad on the ground in the parking lot. I had been airlifted to one of the best trauma centers in the United States.

Luck was on my side that day, since if I had that accident anywhere else on the planet, my injuries would have been fatal. The fact that the accident happened near a school with a large athletic field on which a helicopter could land was a miracle. Also, the fact that the accident was minutes away, by air, from Stony Brook University Hospital, a top trauma center in the United States, was a miracle. This was a grace that I would come to understand later. That was the last time I was here on Earth, in this existence, for what felt like an eternity to me.

Although she was not hit directly, the impact from the accident threw my ex-wife from the Harley. Her injuries were serious, although not life-threatening. She experienced a concussion and several broken ribs, but she was released after a few days of hospitalization. Since I absorbed the direct impact from the truck, I was not as fortunate, and I was in grave condition.

I had a traumatic brain injury, a fractured back, broken ribs, a broken arm, a broken leg, a shattered hip, and many internal injuries, the latter being the most life threatening. Emergency surgery was performed at least twice to stop the internal bleeding. Eventually, my spleen was removed, and I was stabilized. The quickness with which my stabilization had occurred is what saved my life. If the accident had happened anywhere else on the planet, I would have died.

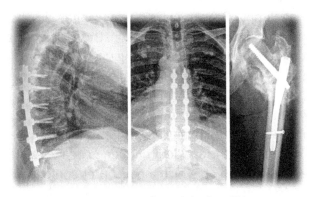

Figure 6 - X-rays of Steve's back and hip.

For the next few weeks, I was kept in a medically induced coma. My back was repaired by stabilizing it with two metal rods. My hip was repaired with multiple rods, pins, and screws. During an office visit several months later, the surgeon said that the surgery I underwent was relatively new and that if this had happened several months previously, the outcome would have been much different.

While in the Intensive Care Unit (ICU) between surgeries, the attending registered nurse noticed that my left foot was cold and realized the lack of circulation could mean that something had to be done immediately to avoid amputation.

My lower leg swelled as a result of the injuries to my leg and my hip, and this cut off the blood supply to my leg. Once again, I was brought in for emergency surgery to save my foot. The surgeon was called immediately to perform a fasciotomy on my lower leg and made two one-foot-long incisions on both sides of my shins to relieve the pressure and restore the blood flow.

The wound remained open for close to two weeks to allow the swelling to drain. The doctors call this injury a self-induced amputation, if not treated immediately. I was on feeding tubes and a ventilator, and it was touch and go for several weeks. The doctors were doubtful that I would even survive. On the outside, I was laying in my hospital bed, but on the inside, I was in another place, a place that I have come to know as "The Place Between Here and There."

Chapter 2: The Place Between Here and There

*"Out beyond ideas of wrongdoing and
rightdoing, there is a field. I'll meet
you there."*

–Rumi

After I left this Earth, I found myself in a place that I call "The Place Between Here and There." By "here," I mean Earth, and by "there," I mean Heaven. The "place between" is like a way station, or what the Catholics would call Purgatory, but it is not a place of condemnation and punishment. It is a place of beautiful opportunities for soul growth prior to transitioning into Heaven or coming back to Earth. Each soul's experience in The Place Between Here and There is tailored specifically to its physical life so that learning can take place. This similarity and familiarity with the soul's previous life allows for a natural transition to occur, so that optimum learning can take place. For this reason, each person's experience would have different settings, although the lessons learned are likely to be the same.

In The Place Between Here and There, time did not exist in the traditional sense. Time had a different meaning. While you are there, time is measured by your experiences, your understanding of those experiences, and your spiritual growth through that understanding. Here on Earth, in this reality that we share, time is measured by days and evenings passing, births and deaths occurring, appointments in the future happening, and the clock ticking. While in The Place

Between Here and There, you review your life on Earth, and you have opportunities to learn from all of your experiences because every experience has a meaning. Time passes when you review your life with the new awareness that you achieve while there. After you have learned all you need to learn, you do not need to be there anymore, and you either transition to Heaven or come back to Earth.

My experience in The Place Between Here and There was centered around three locations which were significant in my life. The first place was a workplace, in which I learned the language of the Universe. The second place was a neighborhood bar and grill, in which I learned the divine connection of all that is. The third place was a local waterfront park, in which I learned about spirit guides and the help that we receive from spirit while we are on Earth.

These three places all happened in sequence. Within each place, I was meant to reach a certain level of awareness. This was gained in what seemed like lifetimes, although the amount of time I was in the coma was only three weeks. When I learned all that I could in one place, I moved onto the next place.

If I had to use a term to describe what was happening, I would say it was a "life review." Each time I gained awareness, I went back to look at my life with my new awareness and could see how I could make things better, how I felt at the time, how others felt at the time, and what every experience meant. With this new awareness, things took on a completely different spin now as they did then. Life made more sense. I understood people's actions and feelings, and I felt incredibly blissful afterwards.

Everything made sense - beautiful sense. I learned that the bullying that I received on the playground helped me to learn to stand up for myself. I learned that the denial of the job I wanted taught me to work harder. I learned that the breakup from the girl that I thought was "the one" taught me that I needed to work on myself before I was able to give to another. I celebrated those moments just as much as I celebrated the moments when I made the baseball team, graduated college, and successfully ran a business, because all experiences are opportunities for soul growth.

In the first setting, the workplace, I was working on computers. I am a computer guy, so solving computer problems was a usual part of my life. Day after day (and I mean that lightly because days in this place were not measured, so I am using the terminology just as a reference), I noticed that the work I was doing was not exactly what I thought it was. There was a deeper meaning behind each computer problem I solved. This relates to the first lesson I learned in this place. What I was being shown was that the computer work I was doing was merely symbolism for life.

Everything that we do in life has a dual meaning - one relates to our existence on the physical level, and the other relates to our existence on the soul level. Life is multi-layered. There are experiences that we have on Earth that seem either too meaningless to bother with or too difficult to bear, yet on a soul level, these are the things that really propel us to higher levels of consciousness.

We choose to come to Earth to have these experiences in the physical world for soul growth and enlightenment, since in the spiritual world, which is our true home, we cannot learn by experience. Earth life is a difficult existence, but it is the one in which soul growth happens most rapidly. Therefore, we cannot have animosity to those who do us harm or challenge us, for they sometimes teach us the most valuable lessons of our lives. Each experience, good or bad, is an opportunity for soul growth on behalf of ourselves and others.

Therefore, we also cannot have animosity towards ourselves either, as we must be able to forgive ourselves for any past indiscretions for which we feel guilt or remorse, since these are also valuable lessons for our soul growth. This may be hard to accept. However, it is essential for soul growth and soul progression. Holding onto animosity toward ourselves and others causes blockages in our spiritual bodies that prohibit growth and contribute to harboring ill feelings that can lead to dis-ease of the body, the mind, and the soul.

We must not judge others, because everyone is on their own spiritual path and will eventually come to spiritual awareness in their own unique time. Feeling spiritual superiority over others, who are not as enlightened as we might believe ourselves to be, inhibits spiritual growth. Rather, viewing others, as well as ourselves, with compassion and understanding is best for all involved, and, conversely, best for the universal consciousness since we are all connected. When you raise your awareness and/or help raise the awareness of another, you also raise the universal consciousness.

Once I realized this, I then reviewed my life with this new awareness, and I realized that all of the "bad" things that happened, were actually beneficial and necessary for my soul's growth. This does not suggest that you should allow people to do harm to you, or that you should seek out negative experiences to fuel your spiritual growth. Rather, when these events do occur, accept them and understand that there is both a purpose and a meaning to everything in physical incarnation.

The second lesson I learned in this place was how to recognize the spirit in everyone and everything. I was working with people in the office that I knew in real life. At first, I saw the people as I had remembered them, which in and of itself seemed a bit odd, because many of these people I had not seen in years and so many years had passed since then. Surely, they would have aged. I then began to see the very same people as children, as teenagers, as adults, and as elders. I learned to recognize them, no matter at what age they appeared to me.

As I became more skilled at recognizing them, the people that I knew as males, I now saw in the female form, yet I was still able to recognize them - not as a man dressed in drag, but as a spirit incarnated in the female form. What I was being shown was their true selves, that part of them that is neither male nor female but is the infinite part of them, which is not part of the physical plane but of the spiritual plane. I could feel their spirits. After a while, I did not even need to see their appearance to know who they were. I simply sensed their eternal spirits.

The next lesson I learned occurred when I began to see the spirit in everything. Everything has a spirit. Everything! There were many human beings that were spirits, but the animals had spirits too. The dogs had spirits; the cats had spirits; the lions had spirits; and the lambs had spirits. As I looked around at the plants, I began to see their spirits. I gazed into the distance, and I saw that the planets and the stars had spirits too.

I began to see spirit, not only in the humans but, in the plants, in the planets, in the animals - in everything. All of these spirits together become the All That Is. We are one. We are all stardust. We were all created in the big bang, in that one moment. Therefore, we are all connected and part of the everything. We each have an individual consciousness. However, together, our consciousnesses join to become the one consciousness of God, the All That Is, the Creator.

The Creator and the creation are one. Our individual consciousnesses are like the cells in a body. There are about 37.2 trillion cells in our bodies, which exist independently and have their own consciousnesses. They live, eat, reproduce, and die. But together, these cells form one body, one consciousness. All souls on Earth form the one consciousness of All That Is - the Creator. These are the lessons I was meant to learn in the first place. After I finished learning these lessons, I moved onto the second setting.

The second setting was a neighborhood bar and grill, a setting I was not unfamiliar with at the time, as I often frequented these types of establishments. I was hired by a man, the owner, to help manage the establishment. There was a woman there, but I was not sure who she was. She spent all of her time praying and had a beautiful and loving energy. My purpose there was to teach a new crop of young souls, that I like to refer to as "the kids," that were recently hired to work there. It was apparent right away that I was not up to the task. Each time the owner told me the assignments that I was supposed to give to the kids, and I went to train them, the kids scattered. They did not even listen to me. This went on and on for a while. I became so frustrated.

It was apparent that the kids were upset that the praying woman was in the bar and grill, although I did not know their reason. Since the kids did not respond to my commands time after time, I thought perhaps the woman's presence was distracting them and inhibiting their progress. They did not verbalize their discontent, but my enlightened awareness allowed me to know they were distraught.

This disturbed me greatly, because I knew that it was important that I complete the task of training these kids, and I was failing. When I was at my wit's end, I went to the bar owner to find out why the woman was there. I figured that if I could do that and communicate the need for her presence to the kids, they would start to listen to me and perform the tasks I gave them.

The owner knew of my plight, since his awareness was even greater than mine. So, he appeared and put his hands on my shoulders. While looking at me lovingly in the eyes, he transferred some of his awareness into me. I noticed the aura around his head. It was brilliant and white. The woman had a beautiful aura too, but when I looked at the kids, they had no auras.

Each time the owner transferred more awareness into me, I became more aware myself. Then when I went to address the kids, they began to listen to me and learn from me. As they learned, their auras started to take shape and eventually grow, and my aura started to increase as well. After seeing these amazing transformations taking place, I realized something quite startling, and this was the first lesson I was shown in that place. That man was me. He was my higher self, that part of me that is always in Heaven.

This higher self is always guiding and teaching us, whether we realize it or not. In fact, our most important teacher is ourself, our higher self. Everyone has a higher self, which is the entirety of their soul, and that higher self always stays as one with the Universe, the source of All That Is. However, when the soul has a physical experience, a portion of their higher self comes into physical existence to learn and grow. Therefore, a soul can be in one, or many more, places at a time. The soul on Earth is always learning from its higher self. Through that guidance and teaching from its higher self, the soul on Earth becomes a teacher to others as well. In life, we are both the teacher and the student.

The next lesson I learned in this place was with respect to the kids. I learned that they were souls that were yet to have a human experience. With my newly imparted awareness, they were learning from me to prepare for their new experience. What was being shown to me was that our souls have always existed. They have no beginning and no end. A soul is eternal. It came from primordial creation. It was not born into its current state. It grows and develops through different incarnations.

The soul greatly desires to learn and grow, and one way it can do that is to experience physical existence. It can learn and grow in spirit, but it takes a great deal longer. Earth life is the fastest way to grow. Further, souls love physical existence, even though they realize how hard it is. We all wanted to be here on Earth to tackle tough lives in order for our souls to grow. We chose this life. We chose these challenges.

The next lesson I learned in this place was that no one was judging my progress. The only one that was judging me was me. Conversely, the only one that was helping me to make progress was me. I was a divine being who oversaw my own destiny.

Therefore, we must not fear a punishing God who would condemn us for our "evil" acts. Whatever we did in life, whether good or bad, was meant to help our soul experience and grow. After we learn from our "bad" experiences, we must love and forgive ourselves and others, because it is the only way to move forward on our path to enlightenment and to help others move forward on their paths. I learned that this path to enlightenment is similar to achieving the Christ consciousness that Jesus achieved. We are all capable of such enlightenment.

Another important lesson I learned is that no one religion has dominion over the other, since we are all here on different paths which lead to the same destination - the divine Christ consciousness, similar to Buddha consciousness, Krishna consciousness, and Yahweh consciousness. We are all here to love one another and help lift each other into this higher state of consciousness

The next lesson I learned occurred when I asked the bar and grill owner why the praying woman was in this setting - what was her purpose? There was a part of her spirit which seemed so familiar to me, but I just could not place it. Also, when I say, I "asked" the owner, I mean telepathically, because all communications are done without actually speaking. In The Place Between Here and There, you "just know" what other souls are thinking, so you do not actually speak.

The bar and grill owner's response was that the woman was invited. It was quite obvious that this was a very unusual invitation and one that does not usually happen in this place. It was also very upsetting to "the kids." The owner said that in this particular instance, she had a purpose here. She was the higher self of a soul who was still in human incarnation but who came here to pray for me. Her prayers were being received and heard.

What I was being shown was that there is an ability to communicate with those who have crossed into The Place Between Here and There and those that have crossed into Heaven. Everyone can speak to their departed loved ones or those in altered states of consciousness. Everyone can pray to those that they believe can give them assistance. Communication never ceases, because consciousness never ceases. After I finished learning the lessons in this place, I moved onto the next place.

The last setting was a scenic waterfront overlook in my hometown, called the Kings Park Bluff. I sat on a park bench there every "day" watching the sunset with two men who were friends of mine in my life. Joey broke his neck when he was a teenager while diving at the bluff. He survived but had a long recovery and required a spinal fusion. He eventually passed when he was hit by a car. John had severe diabetes and as he aged, he developed significant circulation issues which caused infections in his left leg. After one particular infection, he became septic and passed away. Both Joey and John passed away during the year prior to my accident.

Figure 7 - Historic image of the Kings Park Bluff overlooking Sunken Meadow Creek. Photograph courtesy Kings Park Heritage Museum

As I sat on the bluff with Joey and John, we watched and enjoyed the sunset every day. This scene seemed to go on forever and seemed that it would continue to do so, and nothing seemed odd about it at all. However, one day I came to the realization that both of them had passed earlier that year. I thought to myself, how could this be? How could I be sitting here, at the bluff, with my two old friends, if they had passed? This was not possible. But, for some reason, I did not want to ask them what they were doing there.

This went on, sunset after sunset, for many sunsets. As time went by, I felt an urgency building in this setting that something was going to happen soon and that it was going to be big. I did not know what it was, but as each day progressed, the intensity became much greater. Finally, the day came that I knew that I had to ask, or I would forever lose this opportunity to speak with them.

Finally, I telepathically told them that I knew that they had passed, and I asked how and why they were there with me. They simply said that they were there to make sure that I was okay. I did not realize what they meant, because I did not remember the motorcycle accident at that time. This lesson was learned a month after I came out of the coma. When I saw the extent of my injuries and learned that I had a neck injury like Joey and a leg injury like John, I felt their presence was around to help me recover from my injuries. They became guides to me, because they could provide a unique understanding of my needs due to having experienced similar injuries and needing the same type of recovery.

The lesson I learned here was that there are people in spirit that help us while we are on Earth. Just like our higher self helps us, so do spirits that have crossed over. We are always being guided, and not only do we have spirit guides that are with us throughout our lifetime, but we also have temporary guides that help us in certain situations in our life. We have a lot more help than we realize. Therefore, it is beneficial to seek assistance when on Earth and speak to our higher self, spirit guides, saints, angels, and ascended masters. They are all ready and willing to help. By asking for assistance, we can get the answers we need from them and from our higher selves through signs, synchronicities, intuition, dreams, and visions while meditating.

After I learned all that I had to learn in the last setting, I watched the sunset for the very last time with Joey and John. This time, however, as the sun went down, the light kept getting brighter and brighter. It was so bright that I had to shield my eyes. The light was beyond unbearable and way too intense. When I finally was able to open my eyes, I was lying in my hospital bed, and my mother and my sister Sherri were standing over me.

Chapter 3: Why Am I Here?

"Now that I'm here, where am I?"

–Janis Joplin

At first, I did not remember that I was in an accident. In fact, since I traveled from setting to setting in The Place Between Here and There, I thought that this setting was just an extension of my previous experience. I became used to finding myself in new situations, so this one did not seem different at all. Therefore, it did not seem odd to me that I was in a hospital bed, although I could not comprehend why I had so many tubes in me. That seemed ridiculous and unnecessary because in The Place Between Here and There I was fine, and I thought I was still there. So, I wanted to pull the tubes out, but I was tied down and could not move.

My mother told me about the motorcycle accident, which I then only vaguely remembered. She explained how I had been in a coma for three weeks, teetering on the brink of life and death, and how happy she was that I finally opened my eyes. She could not embrace me, since I was hooked up to so much machinery, but I believe my ability to see the spirit in people continued into this life, because I could see in her the amount of love and happiness she felt in that moment. I could also see the love in my sister Sherri as well, in a way that I had never seen before. Her eyes spoke volumes.

 My mother and my sister told me that I would be okay, and I trusted them. They were not going to lie to me. Not realizing the severity of my injuries, however, I wanted to untie myself and go home. I thought that the hospital was just "milking" me for my health insurance payments. I felt fine. I did not feel like anything was wrong with me at all, probably because I was on pain relief medications. Mom and Sherri explained all of my injuries, and it felt unreal to me, since I felt such peace.

At one point, while I was still in the coma, the doctors wanted to give me a tracheotomy. This procedure consists of making an incision at the front of the neck and opening a direct airway into the trachea, allowing a person to breathe through a tube in the throat. Since I had been breathing using a tube in my mouth for quite a while, the doctors felt that it was time for me to stop using that tube. Instead, they wanted to insert a tube through my throat, because they felt that I still needed a ventilator. It was protocol. In fact, the doctors were rather insistent on it.

My other sister Darlene, a respiratory therapist, demanded that they not perform that procedure and instead allow me to come off the ventilator and gradually breathe on my own. She felt that I was strong enough to do so. Darlene knew about the complications and long-term effects of such a procedure due to her job in respiratory therapy. Thankfully, the doctors listened to her, and, with Darlene's help, I was able to get off the ventilator and learn to breathe on my own again. She was an angel to me.

The truth is that Darlene was a brilliant woman. She was an amazing scholar, graduating a year early from high school, and possessing the intelligence to succeed in any profession. She decided to attend a community college and successfully completed a certificate program in respiratory therapy and specialized in direct-patient care. I could not help but think that based on my newfound knowledge of the connection that souls have, she chose that profession because one day it would save me.

Perhaps Darlene was meant to be there in that capacity, in that moment, because she had a purpose in my life. Not that it was her only mission in this incarnation, but, for her to be there at that time, in that critical moment, was miraculous. Without Darlene's intervention, my life could have gone into another direction, and I might not have been in the position that I am today, able to tell and share this story right now.

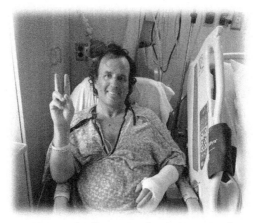

Figure 8 - Steve at the "Step-Down" unit, Stony Brook Hospital

There were several things that felt oddly comfortable to me while I was recovering in the hospital. The beeping of the machinery and all the hospital noises felt so peaceful for some reason. It was like beautiful music. Also, my sister Sherri's voice was completely calming and strangely familiar. I believe that while I was in The Place Between Here and There, I was still conscious of what was going on here. Therefore, the noises in the hospital room were always going on in my subconscious and became soothing to me.

While I was in the coma, Sherri would sing to me, so her voice became part of that peace, as did the voice of a friend named Barbara Williams, who, I later on learned, had prayed over me every day. Being that our souls can be in more than one place at a time, people in altered states of consciousness are aware of what is going on, even in their unconscious state. That is why it is so important to communicate with them. They hear you, and that is why I heard them.

I remained in the hospital for four weeks, then I was transferred to a rehabilitation facility. My physical body progressed rather quickly, considering the doctors thought I would never recover 100 percent. However, it took a while for my spirit to transition back to Earth.

I contemplated that other place and what had happened there. The memories came back in waves, and I was slowly piecing together all that I had learned. Since I never made it to that final place, a.k.a. Heaven, I feel like I was there doing what everyone else who dies does in that place - reviewing their life and getting ready to die. Some people just come back for whatever reason, and I was one of them.

The attending registered nurse was so kind to me, and because I recognized her spirit, I could see how much she cared. It was more than a job to her. She truly wanted to help others. I felt her spirit. She had been taking care of me for quite some time, and I really wanted to talk to her and thank her. It was difficult to speak, however, since I did not have my voice back. In fact, the concept of even speaking seemed strange to me, since I had become so used to communicating with others in a telepathic way. I forgot that people did not know what I was "thinking" and "feeling." The nurse was quite young, so eventually, I mumbled, "For how many years have you been on this Earth?" She laughed, and it made me realize that I see the world differently now than others do.

Being in the hospital was actually a wonderful experience. I was never alone, and I felt love in a way that I had not felt before. Daily visits from my kids, my mother, my sisters, and my brother Scott and his family were more meaningful than they will ever realize. It was as if I had a personal cheering squad.

Friends and people from town also visited frequently, and seeing how obviously emotional they were, to see me in the state in which I was, lifted my spirits and gave me strength. As much as I loved The Place Between Here and There and secretly wished I could go back, the amount of love I received, from all of the beautiful people in my life, made me realize that life is just as good here.

As I recovered, I also started to think about other things in that place. One of my first thoughts was of the spirits - how everything had a spirit, even the animals and the plants. Therefore, I could not bring myself to eat food. It was difficult. Even after I got out of the hospital, it was difficult for me to eat. I eventually drank protein shakes. I would ask myself, "how could I eat a spirit?" It took a while to work through this. People asked me about it, and I declared that "I was a vegan," although I did not really know what that meant, since it was not something I thought about before.

My previous diet consisted mainly of truck stop and bar food like burgers, barbeque, and beer. The first food I ate in rehab was salmon. Something made me feel that eating fish was okay. Maybe it was because Jesus ate fish, or maybe it was because fish do not raise their young and show affection towards their offspring. So, I did not feel guilty consuming salmon. I am not sure why, but, for some reason, I felt okay with eating fish.

I knew I had to eat in order to survive. So, I had to come to terms with this. I started to think about the monkey mind versus the spirit mind. In the monkey's mind, there is survival at all cost, with no remorse and no regret. In the spirit mind, you are without the need of food, since there is a continuation of consciousness no matter what. Since I had just come from spirit, I forgot that I needed to find a happy medium between the monkey mind and the spirit mind, because I was now back to living an Earth life.

Since we are between the worlds, we need to understand that and make the most out of the human experience. We cannot be too monkey-minded, but we also cannot be solely spirit-minded, since we come here to have a human experience. Our bodies thrive best in balance. I still eat mostly plants, but, occasionally, I will consume fish. When I do, however, I take it into me very mindfully with the understanding that the energy - the spirit - is sacred and something with which I must do good.

As I was recovering in rehab, I started to think about the lady in the bar and grill. As I sat in my bed and reviewed my experience, I remembered who she was. One of the things I took with me was the ability to review things based on new experiences and to see spirit. Hers was a spirit with whom I was quite familiar. I knew it was my good friend Kathie.

I felt the connection when I saw her higher self in The Place Between Here and There. However, at that time, it was early in my spiritual development and I just could not reconcile it in my own mind. Once back on Earth, I came to the realization that it was Kathie, and I wanted to talk with her.

Figure 9 - Kathie in the lobby of the Cassadaga Hotel, Florida

My experience in The Place Between Here and There caused me to see people differently. Now that I could see the spirit in people, I found that there were some people in life that were very close to me, but were not connected to me on a soul level, and there were some people who were just friends or even distant acquaintances that were very connected to me on a soul level. You just never know when that connection is going to develop into something important in your life.

Once I came to the realization that Kathie was that soul connection, I wanted to talk with her. The doctors did not want me talking to anyone just yet, so I wrote "phone" on a piece of paper. I figured I would text message her. They told me soon, but not yet, because I still needed rest. I did not want to wait, but I had no choice. I wondered what she was up to these past two months.

Chapter 4: A Communication Beyond

*"To love someone with all of your
heart requires reaching them where
they are with the only words they can understand."*

–Shannon L. Alder, *The Narcissist Recovery Bible*

The days of my friend Steve's hospitalization were brutal, awaiting the news of whether he would live or die. Time slowed to a painstaking pace, and the day of the accident seemed like it was an eternity away. It was the evening of April 19, 2015, and I was happily going about my day unaware of the heartache that was to come.

As a devout nature lover, I was feeling on top of the world hiking in one of the breathtaking waterfront state parks on Long Island. As I was so immersed in the beauty of the early spring foliage and enjoying the fact that the long, cold winter was finally over, it felt like nothing could ever end my momentary bit of heaven on Earth. While in my bubble of bliss, my cell phone rang.

The caller ID indicated that it was my good friend Lisa Titone, who is Steve's cousin. Being my near and dear friend and just an all-around wonderful soul, I gladly interrupted my hike and answered the phone to see whether she called to announce a great outing she conjured up for us (which was possible as she was our friends' group event planner), or if she was just calling with some good news about one of her four kids. They were all in college and were always achieving some kind of success.

Whenever Lisa called, it was always something worth listening to. However, her "Hello" was not the usual cheery one that I normally heard when she called. Immediately, my gut told me something was wrong. "Kath," she said, choking back tears, "Steve was in a motorcycle accident and is in a coma in the Intensive Care Unit at Stony Brook Hospital. We are not sure if he is going to make it." To say I was in shock was a bit of an understatement. I felt like the world just stopped, and I was paralyzed with sorrow and fear.

You see, Steve was a very close friend of mine, and also such a pillar in the tight-knit community of Kings Park, so it seemed impossible that he could ever leave this Earth. His family needed him. His myriad friends needed him. The community needed him. I needed him. He just could not be about to cross over. At the time, my relationship with Steve was purely platonic. He was married with two kids, and I was married with a daughter.

Steve and I met 18 years ago. I was walking my big yellow lab on the property of the Kings Park Psychiatric Center, a popular dog-walking spot. This long-haired, tattooed, Harley Davidson type of guy was approaching me holding a massive German Shepherd on a leather studded leash. Being the typical girl next door type, who loved pink and at the time resembled Molly Ringwald, and not Elvira, I assumed I should nonchalantly walk to the other side of the street to avoid contact. Surely, neither of these creatures would be friendly. Much to my surprise, as soon as I got within shouting distance, this biker smiled and cheerily said hi, while flashing a brilliant, big, white smile. I immediately felt safe and returned the greeting. I then decided not to cross the road.

It turned out that the scary biker guy was actually quite friendly, as was his equally scary dog, and we chatted for quite awhile. We discovered that we both lived nearby and had daughters the same age. I had recently moved to Kings Park, having grown up in Nassau County. I quickly learned that Steve was an expert on all things Kings Park, having been a life-time resident and also affiliated with many local community groups and involved in many town activities. After our initial meeting, we occasionally ran into each other while walking dogs. Eventually, when our daughters entered school, we ran into each other more frequently, since Steve was a Mr. Mom type of guy.

His wife worked nights, and he worked from home, so he was always taking his kids to school, sports, religion, karate, music, and was involved in many school functions. I did not think he ever slept, and I truly admired how much he cared for his children. They always wore nice clothes and had brushed hair, and Steve always had food and drinks with him in anticipation of their hunger or thirst, which is not always a paternal instinct. Steve's children went with him everywhere, whether to school functions, political events, or food shopping.

Our paths also crossed occasionally when Steve gave tours of the Kings Park Psychiatric Center (KPPC), because I attended most of them. He thinks it was because of his charm and charisma, but I know it was because I just loved the creepy history of the abandoned facility, as did the many people that came from near and far to walk the grounds and try to peek inside. I mean, honestly, it is an enchantingly haunting and beautiful place. Who would not be interested in Steve's well-informed tours?

Figure 10 - Kings Park Psychiatric Center, photograph courtesy of King Pedlar

As time marched on, I got to know Steve better and better, since he was akin to the mayor of the town. He was affiliated with the Kings Park Chamber of Commerce, the San Remo Civic Association, the Smithtown Conservation Board, and the Kings Park Heritage Museum. He was also active in local politics, was an elected trustee of the Kings Park School Board and was involved in so many other town activities.

Steve was also dubbed "Captain Video," because he took videos at most of the town sports games, which he posted online for the parents to see. Being that this was before the invention of the smart phone, and videoing anything required the use of rather antiquated and cumbersome equipment, most parents did not videotape their children. We, the athlete's parents, would wait for Steve to do so, and then sign onto Steve's YouTube channel the following morning, in the hopes that he caught our child's hit, touchdown, or goal on video.

He even made videos about town history and the psychiatric center, which were popular on his YouTube channel. Steve was also an avid photographer, a passion which we both shared. We would often post our photographs online and banter over who had the better photographic eye. Therefore, my path crossed with his path often. Everyone's path crossed with Steve's path often, and he was a much beloved Kings Park "Townie," who was rarely at a loss for words.

Figure 11 - Steve and Kathie, circa 2008, Girl Scout Tour of KPPC

When my daughter turned four and I became a Girl Scout leader, Steve was the guy to know. Everyone needs "a guy," and he was mine. I called on him to participate in many of our meetings. There seemed to be a way Steve could help me with most outings for which we needed to obtain badges for the girls' vests. Over the years, Steve gave the girls tours of the local town heritage museum (history badge) and took us hiking on the trails of the psychiatric center (hiking badge). He even arranged for the girls to meet with several local politicians to learn about women's empowerment and local government (politics badge).

As a result, we became exceptionally good friends. We even started a community service group together, called Kings Park Network. Our goal was to get local parks to allow dogs, after our beloved psychiatric center suddenly posted "no dogs allowed" signs on their property. Most of the local parks were "no dog" zones, and being animal lovers, we needed to do something to get our dog walking parks back. During our time together, getting petitions signed and meeting with local officials, I learned that Steve was actually quite kind and caring and not the scary biker dude I feared when we first met.

Steve and I developed a friendship that became sacred because I trusted him. He never acted inappropriately, never looked down my blouse or hit on me, nor did he ever do anything disrespectful. I always knew I was safe with him. Therefore, it allowed me to have a male confidante that I trusted in every way. We also had a nice group of mutual friends that hung out together often, and I just came to consider Steve as one of my best friends. Therefore, when I got that call from Lisa, my heart sank like a cement block spiraling to the ocean floor. Could my dear friend really be departing this Earth?

Lisa explained that if Steve made it through the first twelve hours, there would be a good chance that he would make it through the next twelve hours. And, if he made it through the next twenty-four hours, there would be a good chance he would make it through the succeeding twenty-four hours, and so on. So, she begged me to pray, and that I did, several times each day.

As far as praying and talking to spirit goes, that was something I was good at. After my mom suddenly passed at age 58 of a brain aneurysm, and then my twin brother at age 45 after being hit by a car, I quickly learned to communicate with spirits who had crossed over. I learned that you merely had to ask for messages from them, and as long as you had true belief, they were happy to give the messages to you.

My mother and my twin brother were the two people with whom I had bona fide soul connections. They were my world. Their passings affected me so deeply that I felt as though my soul would be permanently shattered and shuttered. Therefore, I needed to find a way to communicate with them.

I begged my mom for a sign. She always said that she would let me know that she was okay, if she went to the other side. So, I was banking on her to keep her word. It did not take long for mom to appear to me in a visitation. It was the most comforting and beautiful experience of my life and was evidence to me that the souls that you love and the connections you have never die.

Once I knew that I could communicate with my mom, I knew that I could receive messages from other deceased loved ones too. Shortly thereafter, I received messages from my brother, grandparents, uncle, and even an ex-boyfriend who wanted to say he was sorry that he was not as wonderful as he thought he was. Not only did I learn to get messages from them, but I also learned to get messages from saints, angels, and spirit guides on a regular basis. I found that they all returned communication, either through dreams, visions, signs, or synchronicities.

So, I got busy talking and praying to anyone who would listen and begged them to help heal Steve. My "go-to" saint was Saint Jude, who just so happens to be the Patron Saint of Helpless Cases, so it was quite appropriate to ask him for assistance. I knew, for a fact, that Saint Jude was very adept at returning communications.

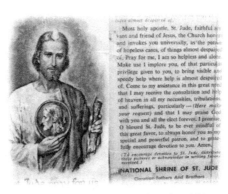

Figure 12 – St. Jude Card Kathie found on hiking trail

I once prayed the Saint Jude novena while walking on an abandoned bridle path at the local park, and as soon as I asked for a sign that he heard me and that everything would be okay, I looked down and found a Saint Jude prayer novena card on the ground at my feet.

Saint Therese and Saint Michael the Archangel were also two saints that I turned to frequently that were really connected to me. They always answered me when I asked for assistance and for affirmations that they heard me praying. Saint Therese sent me roses on many occasions, and Saint Michael sent all kinds of messages as well. With signs like these continually occurring, I knew I had a powerful group of heavenly beings with whom to pray, and I had faith that they would come through for Steve.

I also knew that Steve would be able to hear me talk to him, because after my mom had passed, I also read a lot of books about near-death experiences. These books were great resources for learning what happened to those who had crossed over and provided so much comfort to me when I was in crippling and insurmountable grief. I must have read 20 or more books on the topic. No matter in which decade the books were written, or from which part of the globe, as some books had been from very different cultures, the messages were all very much the same. They all confirmed that there is a continuation of consciousness that occurs when souls exit physical existence.

Through my readings, I also learned that when out of the body, whether a spirit is in heaven or in the state between heaven and Earth during comas, it is fully cognizant and able to hear us. Spirit never dies or loses complete consciousness. Therefore, people in comas can hear every word said to them. This meant that Steve could hear every word that I said to him.

Since I was not next of kin and, therefore, not allowed into the ICU to visit Steve, I began talking to him in my head. "Steve," I said, "I heard about your accident, and I cannot even begin to comprehend it. I am completely devastated. You cannot leave this Earth. You must come back - for your family, for your friends, for your community, and for me. For me - I need you too! I cannot go to the hospital since you are in the ICU, so I am asking you to pretend that I am visiting you in the hospital room. Pretend that I am holding your hand, and that I am praying with you to Saint Jude, Saint Therese and Saint Michael for a full recovery."

I repeated the Saint Jude Novena, a prayer that I knew by heart, and one that I knew to be quite powerful, especially after I found the prayer card on the abandoned bridle path. I also prayed to Saint Therese and Saint Michael for assistance as well. I then told Steve, "We will say these prayers every day until you get out of the hospital." Keeping to my word, I did this every day, several times a day.

After a week went by, I started getting really scared. It was hard to focus on life, imagining my dear friend on the brink of death. I just could not imagine life without him. Then two weeks went by, and I was having tremendous anxiety and trouble sleeping. When three weeks went by, any hope I might have had turned to bleakness. With the passage of this much time, my fear became crippling.

I kept up the prayers, but the word from Lisa was that Steve's time in the coma was getting a bit too long. He was gravely injured, and the doctors were not sure in what condition he would be if he got out of the coma. Would he be able to walk or speak? Would his brain still be functioning properly? It was terrifying!

Knowing the power of prayer, I knew that miracles happened regularly, and with the whole town praying for him, along with me and my trio of powerful saints, I had to keep the faith that we could collectively make a miracle for Steve. Shortly thereafter, to my surprise, I received another phone call from Lisa, although this one came with a much better greeting. "Kath," she said, "Finally we have good news. Steve is out of the coma. I am not completely sure of his condition, but he said that he wants to talk to you as soon as possible."

My excitement was so great that day, as I awaited Steve's call, but it came with a little bit of reservation. For Lisa explained that the doctors were not sure how cognitive he would be after spending so much time in the coma and having had experienced brain trauma. I prayed and hoped for a communication that would indicate 100 percent recovery. The day went by, and I had not heard from Steve, so I sadly went to bed at around 11 o'clock. About ten minutes later, my phone vibrated and indicated a text message from him. I excitedly clicked on the text and read the following message, "Hi Kath, It's Steve. I'm okay. I just want to thank you for visiting me when I was 'out-out,' if you know what I mean."

I was genuinely shocked. I mean, I knew that we could communicate, since I have communicated with those in spirit before. However, one can always question that contact because it is one-sided, since the spirit cannot come back and confirm that you had, in fact, communicated. This message, since it came when Steve returned to his physical self, unequivocally proved that he heard me and that communication with the physical and spiritual planes absolutely does exist. I texted back, "You mean, you know?" He replied, "Let's just say that I've been to a place where I have learned that everyone is connected but that you and I have a connection that goes beyond this Earth. I heard your prayers and your words. And, I know things. So, please visit me tomorrow at the hospital."

I was so excited and went to the hospital early the next morning. I could not wait to hear all of the details about the place Steve had been and what "things" he knew. When I got there, it was hard to believe I was looking at the same person. He was so thin and drawn. He previously was a beefy, muscular guy. The smile on his face and the ease with which his words flowed, however, made it apparent that he did not suffer any major brain damage, although his memory was so-so. That was a relief. I needed my confidante back, and with my life the way it was, I needed him to be completely coherent and rational.

I just sat and listened to Steve for a while, waiting for him to mention the details of his coma experience and the "things" he knew, but he never mentioned them. I did not want to press him, so I just let it go. I figured that he did not say anything because I was with our good friend Pauline, or perhaps that he was just too preoccupied to mention it.

Steve progressed extremely well in his recovery. Having been a man who knew strength training well, he knew how to apply himself and was not afraid to push through pain. His memory remained a little sluggish, but the doctors said he would regain it in time. I figured that was why he did not mention anything about the place he had been while in the coma.

Two months later, he asked if we could go hiking. Steve was just released from rehabilitation, so he was anxious to get his leg strength back. In addition, he was anxious to learn to stop walking like some drunk who stumbled out of the local pub at 4:00 a.m. in the morning.

We hiked a couple of days a week, and Steve started to tell me about his journey in The Place Between Here and There. He did not remember all of the details, but what he did remember was just fascinating. At first, he said he thought it might have been the drugs that made him experience that place, but I emphatically stated that it was not the drugs. If it was, he would not have been able to hear my prayers and my words. I fiercely said, "This was absolutely real, and I experienced part of it too!" It was actually quite annoying that he was so skeptical, especially after this experience. For my entire life, I felt connected to God and spirit and had an unwavering faith in the afterlife, reincarnation, and the limitlessness of the soul. Steve did not really have a spiritual nature prior to the accident, so he pretty much thought I was nuts.

During the next two years, Steve remembered more and more of that place, and he really enjoyed the newfound bits of memory that came to him, because he started to paint a true picture of where he was and what went on there. It was beyond amazing. Steve also regained a lot of his strength. He started eating healthy and exercising regularly. He was back to working full time, and everything was going perfectly. Then, the absolute worst tragedy that could ever happen to a human being happened.

Chapter 5: The Club No Parent Wants to Join

"I still miss those I loved who are no longer with me, but I find I am grateful for having loved them. The gratitude has finally conquered the loss."

— Rita Mae Brown, *Starting from Scratch: A Different Kind of Writers' Manual*

It was the evening of May 17, 2016, and I found my son Nick dead in my basement. I was at home with my ex-wife, as she was recovering from a minor outpatient surgical procedure. Nick's friend came over to see him, so I instructed him to go to the basement which was Nick's usual hangout spot. A few moments later, Nick's friend ran up the stairs and blurted out, "I think something is wrong with Nick; come quick!" I ran right down the stairs and saw Nick lying on the futon. He seemed, for the most part, unconscious, but a slight sound was coming from his breathing, and his eyes were slightly open. I shook him a couple of times, and he was unresponsive.

His mother, a registered nurse, came down and she immediately threw Nick on the ground and began CPR. When that did not help, she went to the cabinet to retrieve a can of Narcan, which she purchased because we had suspicions that Nick was using opioids. When the Narcan did not work, and Nick was not responding, our worlds crumbled as we realized Nick would never be healed and would never walk on this Earth again.

I remember when my ex-wife told me we were having a son. It was the most wonderful moment of my life. I wanted nothing more than to be a father, and I instantly conjured up images of all the wonderful times we would share, from my precious boy's first steps, his first words, his first little league game, his first day of school, his graduation from school, his graduation from college, his wedding day, his first child's birth, and more. I could not wait to hold this little soul in my arms and begin our lifelong journey together.

Figure 13 - Steve and Nick, Little Italy, NYC

It was January 2, 1996 when my ex-wife gave birth to our beautiful 7 ½ lb. healthy boy. We named him Nick, after my grandfather. He had intense hazel eyes and a full head of light brown hair and was a bundle of joy. As he grew, however, it was obvious that he had a rough start in development. He had problems with hearing and was speech delayed. Nick was not developing properly, so we put him into an early intervention program.

The program was minimally helping Nick to develop. Therefore, he was earmarked to be a special education student going into kindergarten. It made me realize that I could not rely on anyone else to devote the time needed to help Nick, it had to come from me. So, I took a few clients from my joint-owned business with my brother, leaving him the rest, and decided to work from home so I could be the primary caregiver to my son, as well as my younger daughter. My ex-wife was working overnights as a registered nurse and was working a lot of hours, so I needed to assume the role as primary caregiver to our children.

I purchased two popular educational programs called, "Hooked on Phonics" and "Hooked on Math," for educational development, and enrolled Nick in karate for socialization, discipline, and focus. I spent a good year totally committed to ensuring that Nick would smoothly transition into the mainstream kindergarten environment. Prior to the meeting to determine Nick's kindergarten placement, I went to an assessment center to get him evaluated. Shortly after Nick went into his assessment interview, the proctor came out and said she would need a tougher test, because Nick had begun to read the proctor's instructions for how to administer the test, up-side-down and from across the room. This was unheard of for a five-year old.

After finding the correct testing materials, Nick was evaluated to have a fifth-grade math level and a sixth-grade reading level. He was also writing long stories using characters from video games that he enjoyed. Clearly, Nick was ready for kindergarten and beyond. I knew that this kid had laser focus and would excel at whatever endeavors came his way.

As Nick's school years progressed, I realized that he, like my daughter, needed emphasis not only in academics, but also in arts and athletics as well. All three "A's" – academics, arts and athletics - are important for lifelong success. With respect to the arts, I thought music would be a great outlet for Nick, and I encouraged him to play an instrument in school. He chose the saxophone, and he quickly became one of the best musicians in the school. He also learned piano and guitar and played both incredibly well. He could play John Coltrane on the saxophone like John Coltrane, Mozart on the piano like Mozart, and Jimmy Hendrix on the guitar like Jimmy Hendrix.

Regarding athletics, Nick initially played football and due to his size and determination, he was a force to be reckoned with. He really enjoyed playing the defensive line with his cousin Victor Titone. He chose number 23 after famed Chicago Bulls basketball player Michael Jordan, and Victor chose number 56 after the New York Giants hall of famer, Lawrence Taylor. Nick and Vic were called "the Twin Towers," because they stood next to each other on the line and towered over all of the much smaller players on both teams.

Nick's true love, however, quickly surfaced in the arena of wrestling. He went on to become a New York State champion and was a celebrated hero in our local small town.

Figure 14 - Coach Jack Magnani and Nick, Kings Park Wrestling

Everything was going great for Nick. Despite the delayed development in his early years, his later years of academic excellence, paired with his athletic and musical success, garnered him a scholarship to Lehigh University. It was a most joyous and wonderful time for Nick and for the family. Everyone was so proud of Nick, and we could not wait to see him take on the world.

Nick's first year of college was challenging. Maintaining the grades necessary to stay in such a competitive school, as well as adhering to the demanding schedule of a Division 1 athletic program, was a lot for Nick to handle. It was clear rather quickly that the stress was getting to him. His grades were failing, and he was losing his focus in wrestling. Shortly thereafter, he had to leave Lehigh.

When Nick returned home, he was obviously distraught, feeling like he did not live up to his personal potential and the potential that everyone saw in him when he initially left home for Lehigh. He did not talk about it, but it was obvious that Nick was intensely changed by what had happened, and there was a general sadness about him. Nick did enroll in a local community college and did well enough to gain acceptance to the prestigious Stony Brook University for physics. However, the melancholy and sadness continued, and my ex-wife and I were seeing behaviors in Nick that were consistent with opioid use. When confronting Nick, he said he was not using anything, but in a very short period of time, it was becoming obvious that this was not so.

When we found Nick dead in the basement, it was the worst feeling in the world. A parent cannot help but blame themselves, and we did our share of that. Personally, I felt that I could have been a better parent. I certainly had an intense love for my children, and they were the number one focus of my life. We did everything together, but sometimes that just is not enough. As a parent, you would like to think that you can be perfect, but it is heartbreaking to admit that there are no perfect parents. We all make mistakes, sometimes terrible mistakes.

I felt like I always encouraged Nick's strengths, when for true balance one really needs to develop their weaknesses as well as their strengths. In hindsight, I felt that I could have encouraged more development in spirituality, empathy, and compassion. It was just so easy to play to Nick's strengths, because they were the things on which colleges truly focused. There are no sections on the SAT regarding spiritual development.

I have since learned the importance of balance from my yoga practice through the work that we do with the balancing of the chakras. Through this practice, I learned that Nick had an imbalance and was governed more by the lower three chakras, which are associated with physicality, and could have used more development in the upper three chakras, which are associated with spirituality. When the upper three chakras and the lower three chakras are balanced, a person lives from the heart.

Perhaps if Nick had more balance, he would not have been attracted to the alternative lifestyle that contributed to his passing. I wish that I had this knowledge prior to Nick's passing and that I had the ability to develop his emotional and spiritual being, in addition to his physical and intellectual being. Unfortunately, that was not the case.

Nick's passing tortured me for quite some time. As I contemplated all that went wrong, and all the "should haves" and "could haves" that came along with it, I also came to another realization that took me by surprise. Maybe Nick went to the place that I went to - The Place Between Here and There - which was a beautiful place of learning, healing, love, and awareness, as well as the place in which you learn that there is a continuation of consciousness. If he is there, since he must be there, then he is happy. He must be happy and full of awareness, enlightenment, and love.

My mind ping-ponged from joy to sadness contemplating all of my thoughts. Thankfully, my friend Kathie was there for me once again during this time and joined me for more long walks during which we talked for hours about my feelings, frustrations, glimpses of hope, and how I can go on amidst this tragic and devastating loss.

The other thing that got me through this dark time was the outpouring of love from the thousands of people who came out for Nick's funeral. Anyone who has planned a funeral can understand how difficult the experience is, but also how comforting it is when you see all of the people who care so very much. I saw the picture of Nick on top of his coffin and was feeling so hollow and emotionless until everyone that knew Nick or that knew our family came through the funeral home door.

There was a line that seemed a mile long down the block. The entire football team and their families came out. The entire wrestling team and their families came out. The entire music department came out. The entire school board came out. The entire chamber of commerce came out. Heck, the entire town came out. Even the people who were on the other side of the political fence than I was came out.

It was the most devastating, yet the most touching, moment of my life. I could tell, however, that those who came to the funeral were grieving differently than I was. I was there grieving my son, and while they were also grieving my son, I could tell in the hollows of their heavy tear-filled eyes that they could not help but imagine that it could have been their child and they were grieving that possibility as well. This was something that I saw in the eyes of everyone I ran into in town for quite some time. I appreciated their concern, but, at the same time, I wanted them to know that I was okay, because I knew that Nick was okay.

Nick went to the same place that I went to – The Place Between Here and There. While I was in that beautiful place, I knew that beyond that realm in which I was, there was a higher realm of love and light. That realm was where those who did not come back to Earth went. Since I never made it that far, I cannot say what was in that place, but I do know that those souls that I came across that were able to travel between the two realms radiated so much more light and had auras the size of rainbows. Nick was in that wonderful place. I just knew it.

Chapter 6: Kathie Shines the Light

"Lighthouses don't go running all over an island looking for boats to save; they just stand there shining."

–Anne Lamott, *Bird by Bird*

After Nick's passing, I knew that I needed to be there for Steve. Losing a child is the worst thing a parent can experience, and I knew that Steve needed someone to talk to and help him from falling into a deep depression. He kept saying that he could have been a better father and was blaming himself, but I assured him that he could not have been more wrong.

What I noticed about Steve upon first meeting him, and what was noticed by all of my fellow mom friends in Kings Park, was what an exemplary dad Steve was. He was always positive and happy, and he had his two kids in tow with him wherever he went. It was obvious how much he loved them and that he would spare no lengths to make them happy. Steve wore his heart on his sleeve, and he needed that big motorcycle jacket-sized sleeve to help hold up such a big heart.

Steve was at PTA meetings, sporting events, town hall meetings, chamber of commerce meetings, and all things community related. He took his kids to religion, music, and sports, and even became a school board member to ensure the well-being of, not only his kids, but all of the kids in Kings

Park. Steve was just that kind of guy. His dedication to the community made him somewhat of a much-appreciated celebrity in town.

Figure 15 - Angel, Dad and Nick, Harley Wide Glide 2001

Honestly, it would have been hard to find a better parent. Of course, though, after something so tragic happens, a parent cannot help but think that they went wrong, and Steve was no different. Because of that, we spent a lot of time walking and talking. Steve poured out his heart and soul and used our conversations to figure out how to survive Nick's passing, while incorporating what he learned about the meaning of life in The Place Between Here and There.

After a few weeks went by, I asked Steve the obvious question, "Has Nick tried to contact you?" He was pretty shocked at my question and looked at me incredulously, as if I was speaking an alien language. I told him that when spirit crosses over, they usually try to contact their loved ones to give them a message that they are okay. Again, he thought I was nuts. Frankly, I thought Steve was nuts, because I figured just about everyone knew about communications from our loved ones who had crossed over.

I told him of several experiences I had with communications from my deceased mother, brother, uncle, and grandfather, but he thought it was all nonsense. I even reminded him of the communications that I had with saints and angels, but he chalked that all up to coincidental occurrences and my active imagination. I would get so mad, because just as I know that the sun is in the sky and that there are fish in the sea, I know that communication with spirit is possible. Further, I would have figured that because he went to "that place" and knew "things," that he would be a true believer of all things spiritual. I could not believe my ongoing talks about spirit did nothing to penetrate Steve's thick skull, nor did his own personal experiences.

When the anniversary of Nick's death came, for five days, everywhere I went, I found roses. The last time this had happened to me was after my brother had passed. The day after my brother's passing, I found a silver heart at the exact area of the hiking trail where I had received the call from my dad about my brother's accident. I then preceded to find silver hearts for the next four days in different locations - one was in the dressing room at Macy's when I was trying on a dress for the funeral, one was sent to me in the mail inside of a sympathy card, one was on a dog walk on the Kings Park Hike and Bike Trail, and one was in front of my house. I just knew in my heart that it was my brother sending love, and this was, in fact, confirmed by two psychics I had seen later on. So, when I found roses every day for five days, I knew it was Nick trying to send some love, since it was the anniversary of his passing.

The roses appeared on the beach at Sunken Meadow State Park, at Caumsett State Park, at Planting Fields Arboretum, at the Fire Island Lighthouse, and on the Kings Park bluff trail. This was surely a sign from spirit, yet doubtful Steve did not believe me. He had a rationalization for the appearance of each rose, chalking it up to coincidence and the fact that "roses are commonly found because people leave them behind after taking wedding photos." That was a new one to me! Anyway, I knew better.

Figure 16 - Roses on the boardwalk bench, Sunken Meadow State Park

People just do not find roses on five successive days, and since roses signify love, I knew that Nick wanted to tell Steve that he loved him and that he was okay. I even explained to him that Nick was probably trying to send messages to Steve himself, but since he was completely blind to them, Nick was trying to reach him through me. I was also sure that Nick was trying to get messages through to Steve's cousin Lisa Titone. We are both two ardent believers in such spirit communication, and when spirit cannot reach the intended party, they try to reach others that can relay their messages.

However, my rantings fell on deaf ears. In my mind, the eureka moment - the final confirmation - came when Lisa had a psychic reading with our dear friend Angela Blanchet and received a message that I thought would be the icing on the Steve Belief Cake. At that time Angela was my friend and had not yet been introduced to Steve, but she knew of Steve as he was akin to the mayor of Kings Park. She knew of his son's passing, as it was big news.

Angela told me to tell Steve that she would give him a reading for free, because she really wanted to help him and because Nick kept telling her that he wanted to talk to Steve. I could not wait to tell him and was furious when he said no. He just was not a big fan of psychic readings. I urged him to go, because I knew how incredible Angela was based on my mind-blowing readings with her. Steve's stubbornness was infuriating.

Lisa had made an appointment with Angela to try to talk to her grandmother, after I told her about my amazing reading. Angela did not know that Lisa and Steve even had a connection, nor did Lisa even mention it. However, the minute Lisa sat down, Angela said that a "Nick" was there and asked if she should allow him to come through. Lisa did not expect to hear from Nick, but it makes perfect sense that she would.

Her son Victor and Nick were cousins who spent a lot of time together, mostly playing football and sports. Both were fabulous athletes that worked out hard and ate healthy, while displaying willpower and dedication that was unsurpassed. Therefore, they had a great deal of respect and admiration for one another and really understood each other well. Victor took Nick's death very badly. He was completely devastated.

Lisa was thrilled that Nick wanted to come through to her, so she gladly told Angela to accept his communication. Angela said that Nick was writing numbers on the wall, 1, 2, 3, 4, 5, 6, and he was circling 12, 23, and 56, and she asked if Lisa knew what these numbers meant. She happily replied that the 23 and 56 made perfect sense since Nick was number 23 on the football team and Victor was number 56, and they stood side by side on the defensive line.

Figure 17- Kathie, Lisa and Victor at the finish line!

Angela then asked if Lisa knew what the 1 and 2 meant, perhaps a birthday, anniversary, or milestone in Nick's life. She could not remember, so she texted me to ask if that was Nick's birthday or death anniversary. I did not know off hand, but I just so happened to have Nick's funeral prayer card in my wallet. When I took it out and turned it over to look at the dates, sure enough it showed that Nick's birthday was 1/2.

Then the psychic said that Nick was saying that he has a synchronicity with Saint Therese and that he is sending the roses. Saint Therese was born on 1/2, and she is known as the Little Flower. Those who pray to her and ask for a sign that she heard from them are said to be showered with roses.

When I heard this, it absolutely confirmed that the roses I found were from Nick and that Saint Therese, one of the saints to whom I often prayed, was conspiring with Nick to get a message to Steve!

I could not wait to tell Steve this news. I was so sure that he would finally accept all my wisdom and apologize for doubting me. I was also sincerely happy that he would know how much Nick loved him and was trying to contact him from the other side. Angela was ecstatic to learn of the connection between Lisa and Steve and was beyond pleased that the message from Nick would finally get to him. She had said that Nick was really trying to get him that message.

The funny thing is, even after this news, Steve was still claiming that all of the messages Lisa received were mere coincidences - that perhaps psychics can read minds or go on Facebook and research their clients. I told him that there was no way that they could research the clients' pasts, because they do not even ask their clients' names, birth dates or any leading information. Also, how could Angela have read Lisa's mind, if her mind was not on Nick, but rather on her grandmother, and that Lisa was not even aware of Nick's birth date.

Angela was such a well-respected psychic and my good friend. Therefore, Steve not accepting this spirit communication was just maddening. I thought I had him there. Even Lisa was shocked, because she knew that Nick was speaking to her too. During her psychic reading, Nick further validated other things that made complete and obvious sense to Lisa and me, and he was spot on about everything. Nick was really trying to get through to Steve, but he obviously needed to work harder, since his father's skull was thicker than the Hoover Dam.

Even though Steve was in total disbelief, I somehow convinced him to help me make a Saint Therese memorial shrine for Nick in a nearby park. We picked a beautiful location - a large oak tree with a split trunk, adjacent to a flowing river, right off the trail head at Connetquot State Park. We brought a statue of Saint Therese and placed it there.

We found a flat piece of wood nearby on which we wrote "Welcome to Saint Therese's Woodland Shrine" and then wrote on a heart-shaped rock, "In Memory of Nick Weber." Steve placated me as I carefully arranged the items, said a prayer, and talked to Nick. He gently held my hand, bowed his head, and then said a few words to Nick as well. Steve thanked me for creating such a beautiful and sacred space for Nick, and I could see in his eyes that he understood the reason I frequented places such as this. They give people a place to be with their sorrow, their grief, and their thoughts, and to transmute those energies to positive energies of love, light, hope, faith, and peace. We left the permanent marker there and some heart-shaped rocks for others who might wish to write memorial rocks also.

Within days, people were leaving messages for their loved ones as well. We were so touched and so thrilled, because it was obvious that others appreciated this opportunity to send messages to their departed loved ones also. We felt that if these messages could help people ease a little bit of their grief, we could also ease ours.

Each time we went, the shrine got bigger and bigger. Therefore, we maintained it impeccably, often leaving a dozen roses in the split trunk of the tree and rose petals on the walkway that we made between fallen logs.

Figure 18 – Saint Therese Woodland Shrine, Connetquot Park, Long Island

On several occasions we ran into people who were praying at the shrine for their deceased loved ones, who also had connections to Saint Therese, and were shocked and amazed to come across this shrine on a random hiking trail. In fact, there were synchronicities and coincidences happening frequently.

When we told our friend Angela, she was so thrilled. Angela also has a Saint Therese shrine in her yard, which was my inspiration for the shrine for Nick. She has also had many communications with Saint Therese, which she beautifully wrote about in her book, *"Kissed by a Rose."* She is an instrumental figure in our lives and, like me, wholeheartedly knows that our connection to spirit is absolute. So, she was not a bit surprised at how powerful our little shrine had become or that the synchronicities and coincidences were occurring. She wanted to contribute to our shrine and gave us a pair of Saint Therese rosary beads and a statue.

On the day that we made the trip to the shrine to place the items there, I took out the rosary beads, as they had been in a package that included Saint Therese's biography. I decided to read the biography to Steve while he was driving. The biography indicated Saint Therese's birth date, 1/2/1873, and then I noticed something completely jaw dropping. "Steve," I said, "you are not going to believe this! Saint Therese and Nick have more than one synchronicity - she was canonized on the day he passed, May 17."

"Come on Steve – out of 365 days of the year, what are the odds that Saint Therese and Nick would share these two dates - the same birth date and her canonization on his death anniversary? Nick said that he had a synchronicity with Saint Therese, and that he was sending the roses. Do you believe me now?" "Well," Steve said, "Maybe there is something to this..." Ha, I finally got him! I called Angela and

Lisa right away to let them know. They could not be more thrilled. Our exhaustive measures to convince Steve to believe were finally over.

Chapter 7: Our Divine Connection

"Bodies meet all the time, but a meeting of the minds, a communion of the souls – this is the uncommon thing."

–R. Queen, *Darkchylde*

Having to admit to Kathie that she was right was hard, because it is always hard to admit when someone else was right, especially after all of her hemming and hawing, but I was somewhat thrilled to do so. Through our recent synchronicities and subsequent experiences, I got to see that all the lessons that I learned on the other side were true. It was not just the drugs, like I initially thought. There is a language that the Universe speaks, and I was becoming fluent in it. If I had to guess why it took me so long to realize it, even after having had the experience in The Place Before Here and There, I would say it was because the topic is still not accepted by all in the scientific community. There is much skepticism from the public which passed down to me.

Since I grew up during a time when the Scientific Method ruled, which meant having to prove beyond a shadow of a doubt that something was real in the here and now sense, I was a natural skeptic. Also, since I did not possess an ounce of spirituality prior to my experience, nor did I hang out in circles that practiced spirituality, I was a hard sell.

Having communicated with Kathie while I was in the coma, having learned lessons that I have found were shockingly similar to lessons other people learned during their near-death experiences, and then having synchronicities happen more and more as time went on, I was now a firm believer in the continuation of consciousness, in the power we have in our own divinity, and that our true identity is our infinite spirit, which was never born and will never die. What a beautiful and comforting realization.

Another beautiful and comforting realization was that my friendship with Kathie was so solid and meaningful in my life. Not many people have friends that exist in different realms of existence, at least not that they know of, but I certainly did. That is why when she told me that she was getting a divorce, it was shocking to me. Here she was, one of my very best friends, and I did not even know.

Kathie told me that she wanted to spare me of her problems when she knew mine were so much greater and that I was the one that needed the attention. Since I was also awaiting divorce proceedings, I thoroughly understood what she was going through.

When I assured her that I could be there for her as well, Kathie explained to me that she and her soon-to-be ex-husband were basically living two separate lives. He was a good man, a good provider, and a good father, but they had been drifting apart for a while. The glue that held them together was their daughter. After she went to college, they realized that they no longer had anything in common. I felt sad for her knowing that she was feeling so disconnected, because I knew that feeling well. It was a classic empty nest syndrome.

For the first time, I saw a different side of Kathie, a more human side. She always covered up her emotions for the sake of others' happiness. Inside, she was a vulnerable and sensitive soul. I wanted to let her know that I could be there for her in her darkest times, because that is what true friendship is all about. After all, she was in The Place Between Here and There, and I knew we had a deep soul connection and were here on Earth to help each other learn and grow.

Never, in a million years, did I ever think that after our divorces, we would become a couple. After all, being friends with someone for 18 years automatically puts you in the "friend zone." Trying to transition from the "friend zone" to the "more than friend zone," is a delicate operation. Neither of us thought it would be wise to do that, since we feared losing our friendship. That would have been a travesty!

It was not until a decent amount of time after proceedings began, that I had a thought, "What if Kathie found someone else, and he did not appreciate our friendship? Then I would lose my friend. I cannot let that happen. I will not let that happen!"

After the demise of our marriages, with kid gloves, Kathie and I did transition from the "friend zone" to the "more than friend zone." It was a process though. You see, I always had a love for Kathie, since we first met. She was such a wonderfully balanced person which was quite refreshing considering all that I had been through. I think everyone falls in love with Kathie when they meet her. She is so caring, so kind, so loving, and so funny.

Since we were both married, not only did I not think of her as a romantic interest, but even if I was single at the time, I just figured that she would be "out of bounds" for someone like me. I just did not fit her squeaky-clean lifestyle. After every encounter with Kathie, I just assumed that she hopped on her unicorn, followed the rainbow, and went home to her pink crystal castle.

I never thought she would be one who could hop on my Harley, blaze down the open road, eat greasy wings and drink beer with me at the biker bar. In fact, when I spoke to my friends and family about her, I always referred to her as Saint Kathie. However, something happened after my visit to The Place Between Here and There and the dissolution of our marriages. I saw the world in a different way. I saw people in a different way. I saw Kathie in a different way. I thought she was starting to see me in a different way as well. We became closer when I became more spiritual.

Being that we were both available now, it was scary to attempt to make the jump to more than friends. It could be wonderful, or it could tank and ruin the friendship. I was scared. I could not imagine her with anyone other than me. So, I had to know. I had to know if she felt the same way.

It was a glorious early evening, and we were taking a hike through Caumsett State Park in Lloyd Harbor, New York. It is truly a magical place, not only due to its location on the beautiful Long Island Sound, but also due to the fact that it once was an impressive 1,750-acre Great Gatsby-era property, with a grandiose estate, a gorgeous barn, a magnificent dairy farm, miles of trails and lush fields, scenic water view overlooks, and a formal walled garden.

As usual, we were walking and talking about our recent divorces, where to go from here, and how crazy life can be. Always seeking the meaning of things, Kathie was mulling over and analyzing why things happened the way they did, what was her mission in life, and if she had disappointed her spirit guides or failed to make them proud.

What I admired about Kathie the most was her desire to be better and to make the world a better place. Personally, I never thought in these terms prior to meeting Kathie, and as exhausting as these self-reflections may be, it felt nice to me to also now ponder my purpose in life and how I can make the world a better place. I recently began to think that maybe Kathie and I could make the world a better place together. I always adored her, but thought that she was honestly out of my league.

Her spirituality was a little intimidating, since it was so different from my "live and let live attitude." The thing is that Kathie was naturally spiritual. It was just in her. She saw the spirit in everyone and was always so positive and joyful. It took no effort whatsoever. I was in awe of that, and I desired to be the same way. I was not a bad guy, but I truly felt that being in Kathie's presence brought out those same positive qualities in me. Her high vibrational energy is contagious, and it truly touched me on a soul level. She made me want to be a better person and to make the world a better place.

During the past few weeks, there were a multitude of signs that made me think that Kathie and I should be more than friends. One of the things that I learned from being in The Place Between Here and There, as well as from initially dismissing the obvious signs from Nick, was that I was not going to make the mistake of not seeing and believing signs again. When these intermittent signs started happening in the presence of Kathie, I began to take notice. I also began to sense that the Universe was at it again. It was a familiar feeling. This was the language of the Universe that I began to know very well.

On this hike, we were in the westernmost part of Caumsett State Park, on a narrow stretch of land that has water on both sides. As we were walking, to our amazement, we came upon a rather large unfinished heart in the sand made of conch shells. Perhaps the tide came in and washed a part of it away, or perhaps the person who made it left it open intentionally. I am not sure. However, there were a bunch of conch shells next to the heart, as if waiting for someone to complete the heart.

Figure 19 - Kathie mending the "broken heart", Caumsett State Park, Huntington, Long Island

Kathie bent down and said, "We cannot leave this heart broken. The shells are within reach. Let's finish this." As she was carefully placing the shells so that the heart was complete, I just knew that there was something to this. This was an obvious sign from the Universe. Why else would this broken heart be here? Why else would the remaining shells to finish it be here? Why else was she speaking of mending a broken heart?

As Kathie carefully placed each shell in the heart, she looked up at me, and I was feeling that I saw love in her eyes. After the heart was complete, Kathie stood up and smiled at me. As she was standing there, the sun was shining directly into her eyes, and they looked more beautiful than ever. I always noticed that when the sun shone directly into Kathie's eyes, they turned a glittery golden color. It was a most unusual eye shade, and I just could not help but become mesmerized by them. As I looked into her eyes, it suddenly occurred to me that I needed to know right then and there if she had the same feelings for me that I had for her.

As I gazed deeply into Kathie's eyes, I just could not help myself. I gently placed my hands on each side of her face, pulled her close, and kissed her. Afterwards, I stepped back and held my breath, hoping she was not gearing up to slap me in the face. She was not. Instead, she looked into my eyes, held me close, and kissed me.

It was the most beautiful, soulful kiss that I had ever felt. In fact, it made me realize that this was the first time I had ever felt love, since what I previously thought of as love did not come close to this – not by a mile. Between this kiss and embrace, our connection and second place was infinity.

In that moment, I knew that Kathie and I were on the path of beginning to make a new life together. Honestly, it was still so mind boggling. I would never have thought we would ever be more than friends, but here we were, fresh from this affirmative kiss. We knew there was no turning back now.

To be truthful, I opened a can of worms. Kathie and I were friends for almost two decades, lived in the same town, had kids the same age, and had friends in common. Surely, if we got together now, people could assume we had gotten together before now. Could they really believe we were just friends all the while? That was our fear, especially since our daughters were the same age. After numerous soul-bearing conversations, we concluded that the Universe put us together. After all, the synchronicities and coincidences meant something. With my new spiritual awareness, I knew that. It was Kathie's poking and prodding that helped me to understand how these signs from the Universe worked in the first place. Therefore, she knew it too.

We decided to tell a few of our closest friends. They were all thrilled and said they always thought we would make the perfect couple. Eventually, we became an official couple, and everything worked out beautifully. I am sure the Universe made sure of that, and I am sure that is why Kathie's higher self was in The Place Between Here and There. Her higher self was there to make sure that I was coming back to Earth, because we were meant to be together.

The Universe validated this fact once again, when we revisited the site at Caumsett State Park where Kathie completed the heart of conch shells. To our amazement, there were a dozen beautiful white and yellow roses in the exact location. Someone would have had to traverse a long way to place the roses there, as they were miles from the parking lot. It was a magical moment.

Figure 20 - "The Roses", Caumsett State Park, Huntington, Long Island

Once that spiritual door is opened and you acknowledge the signs and synchronicities, they multiply in the most joyous ways. There was nary a day that we did not have a sign from the Universe, and that helped us to believe in our union. We had a higher purpose, and I was about to find out what that was.

Chapter 8: Emergence of the Inner Teacher

*"Everybody is a genius. But if you judge
a fish by its ability to climb a tree, it will
live its whole life believing that it is stupid."*

–Albert Einstein

Kathie kept telling me that I should speak of my near-death experience, because she felt it would be beneficial to those who were grieving or to those who would just appreciate hearing the lessons that I learned in The Place Between Here and There. She begged me, in fact. Truthfully, I did not want to do that. First, I thought, "Who would want to listen to me? Who am I that anyone would care about my story or want to hear about it?"

Yet, each time we met people with whom we felt comfortable enough to tell the story, they were fascinated and comforted by it. This surprised me, although it did not surprise Kathie. She got pretty good at saying, "See, I told you so." Yet, I was not ready to go public, and Kathie patiently waited without hounding me too much. She believed in divine order and figured I would come around some day, and she also knew I was still a novice on the spiritual path, even though The Place Between Here and There catapulted me into a new awareness that normally took people years and years of dedication and study.

Being that I was now on this spiritual path, I decided that I needed more spiritual activities in my life. I figured I might as well take the bull by the horns and run with it. Yoga was something that kept popping into my mind, my news feed, and my conversations. Therefore, it piqued my interest. I decided to search online for local spiritual yoga practices, and a studio called Kundalini Yoga of Long Island was the first entry. This studio is in Northport, which was only a few miles away from where we live. I read the information on the studio, the teachers, and the philosophy, and felt that this was something that would be beneficial to try.

When I asked Kathie if she wanted to join me for an introductory class, she responded that we had too many things to do already and that she did not want to get involved in any new endeavors at this time. However, when I told her that I made a reservation for the Tuesday night class and that I would check it out and let her know how it was, she remained silent for a minute. Then she blurted out, "Wait, you and ten women together in a yoga class, in form-fitting yoga clothes, doing downward dog and other funky positions... Nope, I don't think so. I'm going too!"

So, together, we ventured into this unchartered new territory, and we were immediately blown away. First of all, neither of us had done any yoga previously, so while we expected a physical practice, we did not expect the level of spirituality and the wisdom and connection to consciousness that comes from Kundalini yoga. It resonated beautifully with what we had learned regarding my experience in The Place Between Here and There. Also, we met some of the most wonderful people in this present incarnation on Earth.

Within days, we signed up for the unlimited monthly membership and then attended every workshop and concert offered as well. Kundalini yoga is a blending of physical and spiritual practices, which causes a balancing of the chakras, a connection to divine consciousness, and a connection to all that is. This is similar to what happens when in The Place Between Here and There, except that you do not need to experience a near-fatal accident to get there.

Figure 21 - Teaching Staff at Kundalini Yoga of Long Island – Annie Morgan, Theresa Banks, Lee Knight, Iris Eplan and Teresa (Madam) Devine

Through meditation, mantra (chanting), pranayama (breathing), and asanas (exercises) that work on the ten bodies (soul body, negative mind, positive mind, neutral mind, physical body, arcline, aura, pranic body, subtle body and radiant body), kundalini yoga can elevate your consciousness to a divine level which leads to peace and bliss. It is the perfect recipe for dealing with the challenges of life and with accessing your inner teacher - your higher self.

Kundalini yoga became a six-day per week practice for Kathie and me. Not only did we attend regular classes at the local studio, but we also attended a myriad of workshops, festivals, meditations, and chant artist concerts. After devoting the past two years to learning all we could about the spiritual aspects of this form of yoga, it was apparent that there was a tangible correlation between Kundalini's teachings and what we learned about The Place Between Here and There.

Although Kundalini yoga is not a religion, it is a means by which you can connect with the energy of your being, your divine self. Whether you are affiliated with a specific religion, or none at all, Kundalini yoga's philosophy is that we are all one, under one Creator. It is a connection directly between you and the Creator. There is no intermediary, no guru, yogi or swami standing between you and the Universe. It is an inward practice that connects you with All That Is. This was especially attractive to me, because in The Place Between Here and There, I learned that the divine teacher is inside of oneself, and all you need to do is to let your spirit lead the way.

In fact, most of the Kundalini mantras (chants) predate all modern religions. What we learned in Kundalini yoga is that our spirit is here to learn to remember its divinity. The exercises, or asanas, in the yoga practice strengthen our physical and mental bodies so that we can handle the challenges that are necessary in life. These challenges help us attain higher enlightenment. They are like warm-ups or practices before ball games. The mantras we chant are affirmations and praises that help us elevate our consciousness so that we can maintain a high vibration and become beacons that shine love and light to all beings. This is the same state of being which you feel in The Place Between Here and There, a feeling of continual love.

The meditations we do enable us to go within, connect with our higher selves, and achieve higher states of awareness (those moments that allow us to continually expand our consciousness and achieve soul growth). This realization of awareness is why we are here. Since our soul is eternal, it always has been and forever will be. It will perpetually seek spiritual growth. This will happen lifetime after lifetime after lifetime, until we become fully enlightened beings.

While attending many of the Kundalini yoga practices and workshops at the yoga studio, the topic of "the soul" was a repeated theme. Feeling that I understood the soul, based on my experience in The Place Between Here and There, I was always confident and vocal at expressing my ideas and the lessons I learned while there. These comments always garnered a surprisingly decent amount of interest from our fellow yogis. As a result, Kathie again suggested that I share the details of my experience in a workshop at the studio, since now we found an audience that was amenable to such a discussion.

To say I was apprehensive was an understatement, because I still felt like I did nothing to deserve this podium. There were people in the community who spent a lifetime, perhaps many lifetimes, learning about spiritual development and dedicating their lives to education on the topic. Yet, here I was, a previously nonspiritual pleasure maximizing unit, who just had the luck to survive a near-fatal motorcycle accident, which caused my enlightenment. Therefore, who would want to listen to me.

Kathie insisted that it was not luck and that people would love to listen to me. She told me that I was chosen by spirit to have the experience, because I was a seasoned public speaker, who could convey a message to others in a dramatic and emphatic way. She also told me that the fact that I lost my son, and that I was able to go on knowing that he was in that beautiful place of enlightenment, further ensured that this was a story that needed to be told. Everyone on Earth grieves someone, and some are even paralyzed by their losses.

Kathie felt that I could help people see that life is eternal, that spirit is always connected, and that living on Earth is a beautiful experience to treasure at all costs. Thick-headed as usual, I remained unconvinced. Kathie said, "Steve, you might not feel worthy of speaking about this for the reasons you state, and I get that, but sometimes God chooses the most unlikely of servants. Please consider doing this at some point, because you need to spread this message of hope and love, and the sooner the better!" She was not about to give up the fight.

What it finally took to get me to change my mind and finally take the podium was a desire to send a cash-strapped 85-year old yogi friend to Sat Nam Fest, an amazing week-long yoga festival in the Berkshires, Massachusetts. We met this beautiful lady, Nancy, at our first yoga class. She beamed like the brightest ray of sun and radiated love and light like no one we had ever met before. In addition, her wisdom about all things spiritual was the most impressive we had ever seen.

No matter what anyone was talking about, whether it was the meridians in the body, Rumi verses, planetary alignments, numerology meanings, or yoga pose benefits, this woman knew it all. It became a joke after a while, because when a teacher or speaker was discussing any topic at all, Nancy would raise her hand and add her bits of knowledge that just blew everyone away. We would all look at each other and say, "Of course Nancy would know that!" To say she was also a seasoned yogi was an understatement.

Figure 22 - Nancy's 85th Birthday at Kundalini Yoga Long Island

The woman, mind you in her mid- 80's, could hold any position for as long as was demanded, and that could be for an excruciatingly uncomfortable amount of time. Her abs were rock solid, and her arms could hold the weight of the world. How she fit all that power into a size zero body was beyond anyone's belief.

Nancy was a yogi when yoga was considered a new fad in America. Born in 1934, Nancy was in her prime by the time the hippie movement came and when yoga started a boon in America. She moved to New Mexico to be immersed in the spiritual scene and obviously remembered everything she ever learned. Being in Nancy's presence was like being in the presence of the light. Her optimism and fortitude, as well as her beauty, made everyone want to be her student, for she was a guru, a master, a teacher. That is why we were heartbroken when the annual Sat Nam Fest yoga festival came around and Nancy could not afford to go. Nancy needed to go. People benefit from her presence, her knowledge, her optimism, and her light. She just needed to be there!

We brainstormed - how can we raise money for Nancy? Kathie suggested a yoga fundraiser with a Chinese auction, raffles, and free yoga classes or healing sessions, but I just was not resonating with those suggestions. Without even thinking, I blurted out, "How about we do a workshop on The Place Between Here and There, and we can use all of the proceeds to send Nancy to Sat Nam Fest?"

Obviously, since Kathie had been hounding me for the past two years to do such a workshop, she was beyond thrilled and agreed without hesitation. Not only was she thrilled that I would publicly tell of my experience, but she was thrilled that we could help Nancy. This was a win-win.

I now look back at all the messages from the Universe that were so blatantly obvious that I should tell this story. Kathie was unwavering in her position. The signs and synchronicities were constant, but I was just not open to them. I wonder how many people are also getting signs from the Universe but are closed off like I was. The Universe is constantly speaking to us, and as soon as we learn to understand that language, life blossoms like the most exquisite flower.

We are meant to be connected to the spirit realm just as much as we are meant to be connected to the physical realm. We are the conduit between the two with energy flowing equally in both directions. After learning this, and acknowledging the synchronicities that occurred, I felt renewed. I wanted to shout from the rooftops and was more than happy to agree with Kathie that we needed to tell the story of The Place Between Here and There.

Once we put on our workshop hats, everything just ran so smoothly that we absolutely knew we were divinely guided. Timing is everything, and this was obviously the time. Our dear friend Theresa Banks, the owner of Kundalini Yoga Long Island, offered the use of her studio to do the workshop and said that she did not even want a percentage of the ticket sales, so that all the proceeds could go towards Nancy. It was such a beautiful gesture. We were overwhelmed but not surprised by this generous offer. Theresa was our first Kundalini teacher, a most beautiful soul, and also a dear friend to our beautiful Nancy.

The amazing community of light-bearing yogis at Kundalini Yoga Long Island were our lighthouse through the fog of our most challenging times. So, it came as no surprise to us when this community learned of our endeavor to help Nancy, and everyone came out to attend and provide generous support. The workshop was an overwhelming success, and we raised every cent needed to send Nancy to Sat Nam Fest.

Figure 23 - Theresa Banks presenting Nancy with Tickets to Sat Nam Fest

What I did not expect out of the workshops, although "Little Miss I Told You So" knew it, was the sheer amount of positive feedback we received afterwards. Kathie was right. People grieve, either publicly or silently, and that grief creates such an abyss and pain in their hearts. It makes them question whether God exists at all or what is the purpose of life. Prior to my experience, I thought about those things as well, although they did not debilitate or consume me.

Had I not had that experience in The Place Between Here and There prior to my son's death, however, my outlook would have been extremely bleak. But, now, unequivocally I believe in the continuation of consciousness, the eternity of the soul, the necessity of life experiences - good or bad - in the attainment of spiritual enlightenment, and the bliss that is achieved by having these experiences. Being able to help people understand and accept this new reality was a blessing and a gift, and it was a way in which I could honor my son's passing.

Figure 24 - "Between Here and There" Workshop at Family Tree Yoga, Nesconset, Long Island

We hosted five very successful workshops even after we made enough money for Nancy to attend Sat Nam Fest. Further monies were put into a new foundation we began to provide yoga scholarships for seniors and young adults.

At first, I thought speaking of my son's passing would be difficult. However, once I saw how much others were moved by my experience in The Place Between Here and There, and how that experience helped me survive after losing my son, as well as how moved people were when Kathie got up and spoke about our relationship and our communication across the ethers, I knew we had to continue sharing the story with others.

It felt good to be helping others, and we were spiritually learning and growing through these workshops as well. My physical body was still on the mend, but I was working just as hard at growing spiritually as I was at recovering physically.

Chapter 9: The Recovery Process

"The wound is the place where the light enters."

–Rumi

The physical rehabilitation of Steve was nothing short of a miracle. He defied all projections of a less than full recovery, and became the Six Million Dollar Man, due to both the amount of hardware in his body and the amount of recovery and strength he achieved after his impressive hard work. I must admit, however, I did enjoy my temporary ability to be able to kick his butt, and it came in handy at times – many, many times.

Steve's stellar improvement did come with a bit of struggle. He was never one to follow researched and proven directions of highly educated medical professionals. Of course, my articulate and caring suggestions to Steve to listen to the doctors and follow through with physical therapy fell on deaf ears, even though I made less than delicate suggestions that he resembled Frankenstein when he walked.

Steve had this innate law of attraction positivity and was convinced that he could heal himself through exercise, since he had been working out for most of his life. He was a rather muscular guy prior to the accident, and I am sure that under his slight beer and hot wing belly were some killer six-pack abs. Yet, due to the muscular atrophy that he experienced after the accident, he more resembled a plucked chicken, rather than The Rock.

Figure 25 - Steve before and after accident – Left photograph by Lou Varrialle, Right Photograph by Joann Crowley Beckman

I did not agree that Steve's prior experience in the gym qualified him to rehabilitate himself after a severely injurious, near-fatal motorcycle accident. However, Steve was not manager of the normal department, so we commenced his deviation from the medically recommended rehabilitation protocols. I begrudgingly agreed to join him on hikes and encourage him as he began working out again, even though I truly thought he should take it a little more slowly.

In retrospect, I must kick myself for doubting Steve's law of attraction ability to manifest total recovery. After all, I read *The Secret*, and I know that positive thoughts create a positive reality. My own personal experiences proved that. I guess I just felt that the degree to which Steve was injured was devastatingly grievous, so he should not be too overconfident that he would fully recover. He proved me wrong. I think Steve enjoyed the fact that he taught me something for a change, since I was the one who usually assumed, and rather enjoyed, the mentor role in our friendship. I just stood by and watched the amazing transformation of Steve The Plucked Chicken to Steve The Rock.

As he went into full-force, psycho rehab mode, Steve was convinced that each day he felt better and better and that he looked forward to waking up in pain because, "it was a wonderful opportunity for improvement." His positive attitude was admirable, although I was still sure he was being a bit of an ignoramus.

Being that I tore my ACL playing tennis five years prior and rehabilitated wonderfully through the normal method of physical therapy, I felt that Steve should have given it a shot, even for once-in-a-while guidance. But, no, not Mr. Smarty Pants. As a good friend, however, I supported Steve, and applauded his small victories – first in eliminating his Frankenstein-like walk, and then in endeavors more challenging than walking erect, like gaining muscle, strength, stamina, and speed. Steve did it all.

Steve even graduated from short hikes on the flat trails at the Kings Park Psychiatric Center to hours-long rather challenging hikes on the nearby uber-hilly hiking trails. I always held in my laughter when Steve had a momentary Frankenstein relapse and tripped on a root or a rock, although he was not as kind and almost died laughing when I slipped in a mud puddle because of what he deemed to be my "inappropriate" footwear. To this day, he still giggles like a schoolboy when recounting this extremely unfunny event.

Mr. Positivity became a devourer of challenging workouts, pushing himself to limits that I could hardly believe. Knowing that I was a runner and could be a helpful running coach, Steve even made a declaration that he wanted to run the Kings Park 15K race, a rather difficult local race that is 9.3 miles long, extremely hilly, and not for a novice runner nor for a man who just got his bell rung. I suggested that he start with an easy and flat 5k, which is a 3.1-mile run.

Not being one to take baby steps, Steve said that he needed to reach for the stars otherwise life would not be worthwhile. So, we trained. Well, I was already trained. I trained him, which honestly meant that I had to run very slow for a while, but it was wonderful to witness Steve's progress. Not only did he run that 15k, but we ran many other 15k's, 10k's, and we even ran a half marathon.

Figure 26 - - Claudia Kirk, Steve and Kathie crossing the finish line at the Kings Park 15K – Photograph by Sue Robinson

A big boost to Steve's ability to progress during his rehabilitation with hiking and running was the inclusion of a Fitbit tracker. A Fitbit is a wonderful device that you wear, like a wristwatch, that tracks your steps, calories, miles, and heart rate, among other things.

While this device keeps count of your steps, the accompanying smartphone app allows you to join challenges with other fitness-minded people, who compete for the highest number of steps. Steve and I both got Fitbits and joined a challenge group of ten people. We were mostly strangers at first, but we became good friends who supported each other, pushed each other, and egged each other on in such a way that we were all vying to be the winner of each daily and weekly challenge.

This camaraderie was instrumental in Steve's recovery, as the all-day banter in the chat pushed Steve to go out and do as much as he could to become the winner of each challenge. Steve would get so many steps sometimes that we would all joke that he probably put his Fitbit on the ceiling fan while he was resting, although we knew that he did not. Truth be told, Steve stepped his butt off. He exercised before work, during lunch, after work, and all weekend long. Where there is a will, there is a way, and Steve's will was to recover 100 percent from his accident, and he was at about 75 percent.

Steve's doctors were shocked. They did not think he would ever be able to accomplish anything more than barely existing, never mind running a half marathon and bench pressing his weight. But even with these grand achievements, Steve's body still was limited with some movements, and he was not going to accept that. It was actually through Kundalini yoga that his body completely rehabilitated to 100 percent. When we first began yoga, it was very challenging for Steve. Yoga poses are hard enough for an agile person, never mind a person with rods, pins, screws, and plates up and down their back and legs. Steve was determined, though, and gave yoga his all, just like he gave everything else his all.

At first, sitting in easy pose, also known as "Indian style" or "crossed leg" position, was the hardest task of all. Steve's body just did not want to twist into that position, especially for long periods of time. Once he was somewhat adapted to easy pose, Steve conquered other yoga challenges like touching his toes, sitting on his heels, and downward dog, among many others. It was through the daily stretching of the muscles and the dedication to the practice of yoga that Steve made the most significant strides in improving his physical body, not to mention his mental body and his soul body.

Theresa Banks and the yoga teachers at Kundalini Yoga Long Island, and Tina Marie Bertoli and the yoga teachers at Family Tree Yoga, were remarkable during Steve's rehabilitation process. It is said that "it takes a village," and it took these yoga studios' villages of kind and caring teachers and students to transform Steve from Frankenstein to a yogi.

They celebrated each of Steve's milestones with such fervor and genuine compassion, which truly inspired him to push even harder. Again, in my opinion, he pushed too much, attending yoga every day and sometimes more than once a day, but Steve was going to do what Steve wanted to do and not what wise Kathie told him to do.

After two years of yoga, Steve was back to almost full strength. In fact, he was doing things that he could not even do before the accident. Not only was his success due in part to his dedication to physical rehabilitation, but his experience in The Place Between Here and There gave him a perspective and an advantage that most people do not have.

Steve learned that things happened for a reason and that it was in his best interest to learn from those things. He also learned that he had spirit guides and help from Heaven. In the case of Steve's physical rehabilitation, this was channeled guidance from his friends John and Joey. He felt they were there to "make sure he was okay," and he sensed their presence and love during his recovery. Steve also learned to appreciate every experience in his life and to enjoy the journey just as much as the destination.

Chapter 10: Jesus Sent Me

"Very truly I tell you, whoever believes in me
will do the works I have been doing, and they
will do even greater than these, because
I am..."

John 14:12-14 NIV Bible

I must admit that even after doing many successful workshops and a television appearance on the story, I still felt a bit unworthy of the podium. I guess that in a world of eight billion people, it is hard to believe that I could be a likely servant to deliver a message to others. Kathie's belief in me, and my love for Nancy, gave me the ability to speak about my experience. I recalled an encounter that took place many moons ago, that did not seem to be very significant at the time, but I now felt was a precursor, or better yet a synchronicity, for what was to come.

After retiring from her job as a social worker, my mother moved from New York to "The Villages," a very active retirement community in Florida. An extraordinarily brilliant and beautiful woman, it was always a joy to go and visit her. I was ashamed to admit, however, that it was well over a year since I had seen her last, so this trip was long overdue. We spent the entire time going from place to place, activity to activity, and keeping up with this energy extraordinaire was not easy. I did manage, however, to occasionally sneak out and get some sun and $1 malted beverages at The Villages Brewery, while mom went to bridge and the foreign film club meetings.

Sometimes, you need a vacation to recuperate from a vacation, and that is pretty much what I needed after this trip. I was exhausted when I got to the airport for my flight home. Due to that exhaustion, coupled with a mild dehydration from the sun and spirits, I was truly looking forward to my mile-high, three-hour snooze and could not wait for the announcement of the boarding of my flight.

My head was pounding when I finally boarded the plane and arrived at my assigned aisle seat in row twenty-two, which I later learned happens to be an angel number. After a bunch of delays, due to local thunderstorms, it felt like heaven to finally be seconds away from my snooze. I glanced over to see with whom I would be sharing an armrest for the next few hours.

It was an older Hispanic lady, shaking, clutching a rosary, and mumbling something in Spanish. Seriously, that was the last thing I needed. Not that I was not a caring and compassionate person, but I just needed to rest, and dealing with this lady just was not on my itinerary.

To distract myself from her nervous jitters, I placed earbuds in my ears and began searching my playlist for something to transport me to dreamland. Just then, the cargo door closed and made a loud sound. When the lady heard this noise, she shrieked and started praying at a higher volume. Her shaking also worsened, as I felt from our shared armrest. I opened my eyes and took a quick glance to notice that her eyes were beginning to water.

I had a feeling that this would be the beginning of an hours-long ordeal. I just wanted her to shut up and calm down before things worsened. I know that sounds a bit harsh, but I was just so very tired, and I was also somewhat less spiritual and less emotionally evolved than I am now.

I had to think of something. Her hand was clutching the armrest for dear life. I do not know why, but I instinctively reached out and held her hand. This startled her, and she looked at me with a somewhat frightened look. I thought she might even shout out for help, thinking I was groping her. I began to become a bit concerned myself. Again, I did not know what to do and had to think of something.

I held her hand a bit tighter, looked into her eyes and said, "It's okay, Jesus sent me." I am not sure why I said it. It just slipped out. Immediately after I said it, I felt so guilty. I would not have been surprised if a lightning bolt came down from the sky and struck me dead in that moment. I thought it was especially cruel that I tried to mislead her, an obviously devout religious person, while I was, at the least, an agnostic.

Just then, however, the most amazing thing happened. The lady half smiled at me and mouthed in English, "Thank you." She was still very scared at this time, but the shaking and chanting stopped, and the situation was becoming somewhat more manageable. I was even starting to feel a little bit better about my "Jesus sent me" comment.

When the engines roared to life and the aircraft started to move, she went back to shaking, sobbing, and praying all over again. This time, it was even worse. She began squeezing my hand so tightly that I began to question the wisdom of holding her hand in the first place. I was completely at a loss for what to do next. There was no way I could turn back the clock because I owned this now. So, I shrugged my shoulders, raised my eyebrows, leaned over and said, "Do you have any grandchildren?"

Well, the "Walls of Jericho" came tumbling down after I asked that question! In perfect English, she told me that her granddaughter, Maria, was getting married to George, and that was why she was on the plane. She explained that this was the first time she had been on an aircraft and that she did not like it at all. She might not have liked the airplane, but she certainly liked to talk. She then went on to tell me that George's real name is Jorge, and she does not know why he needs to use George instead of his given name, but she is not going to be too critical because her married name is Bernstein. When she tells people her last name, they roll their eyes and smile.

She told me that Maria makes more money than George, which seems very odd to her, but she understands that times are different now. The lady explained that she came to this country on a boat (or more like a raft) from Cuba, back in the late 70's, so that her children and now grandchildren would be able to make choices for themselves and have opportunities. She went on to say that she is not going to be judgmental. "Jorge, I mean George, is a good fellow, and he and Maria are in love, so I know they will be happy."

She went on for two and a half hours, without coming up for air once. When the aircraft took off, she did not even notice. As the landing gear loudly clunked back into place, she did not even notice. As the chime rang to indicate cruising altitude, she did not even notice. As the landing gear lowered and the aircraft touched down for a landing, she did not even notice. She just kept talking and talking, with obvious love in her eyes for her family and an ease in her manner that was completely counter to when I had first sat next to her.

By the time the aircraft taxied to the gate, I knew almost everything a person could know about a family without meeting them. I came to realize that this lady had experienced so much life, both the good and the not-so-good, and she was okay. Actually, she was more than okay. She was happy and wise and understood what life was about and the beauty that surrounds us all. She expressed that we all have so much in life for which to be grateful, and that we should always be willing to love and to be loved and to think positive thoughts, because those things are the keys to happiness.

When it came time to depart the plane, she could not reach the overhead bins, so I retrieved her bags and carried them off the aircraft. We walked down the long ramp together, and, as we did, I was once again feeling guilty about the "Jesus sent me" thing. I had come to know her and had strangely developed a deep love and respect for her. Therefore, I felt the need to level with her and tell her the truth. In the distance, I could see a large crowd of people standing at the end of the secured area near the baggage claim. I knew from her descriptions that this was her family, and standing at the head of the gaggle were Maria and George.

I pulled her aside that told her that I did not want to intrude on her greeting with the family, so I wanted to say goodbye now. I placed her bags down next to her, took a deep breath, and said quickly in one breath, "I have something I must tell you. I lied." She looked perplexed, and as her forehead crinkled with concern, she asked me what was wrong. I explained to her that Jesus did not send me. I honestly explained, "I just wanted you to shut up. I was tired and cranky and just wanted to rest. You were making so much noise, and I wanted you to stop."

Surprisingly, she let out a big laugh and clapped both of her hands together. She then reached up, placed a hand on each one of my cheeks, pulled me down, and kissed me on my forehead. She then looked me straight in the eyes and said, "The only one you misled was yourself. Jesus did send you." I quickly shook my head and said, "No he didn't. I'm not even religious." She smiled and let me stand up straight, took both of my hands into hers and said, "Jesus sometimes chooses the most unlikely of servants, and, once again, he chose wisely."

I watched her as she reached the end of the gate to greet her family. Before they all walked away, she turned to me, smiled and mouthed the words, "Thank you." And, I thought about what she said, "Jesus could not have chosen a more unlikely servant than me, and once again, he chose wisely," and that maybe she was right. Despite my exhaustion and need for rest that evening, the life lessons I learned on that flight and from such an unlikely source will stay with me forever. I guess Jesus chose us both wisely.

I really wish I could see the lady on the plane one more time to thank her for our meaningful discussion and for her kind words. These words, so similarly synchronistic to the ones that Kathie used when trying to convince me to tell of the experience, "sometimes God chooses the most unlikely of servants," truly helped me see myself as a worthy messenger of this story. Further, my love for Nancy, my beautiful soul family member, and my desire to have her with us at Sat Nam Fest, also helped.

Sat Nam Fest was glorious. We spent a week with our soul family, Nancy, Kathie's daughter Kristen, her boyfriend Sean, and all our friends from Kundalini Yoga Long Island, doing yoga, attending amazing concerts, eating delicious vegan food, and meeting wonderful people. As expected, Nancy was a magnet of love and light to all the beautiful souls with whom she made contact. She was a "rock star" in every way, shape, and form. We knew she needed to be shared with others, and we were so happy to see how much she enjoyed Sat Nam Fest as well as how much Sat Nam Festers enjoyed Nancy.

The Universe does work in magical ways, and during Sat Nam Fest, I had the opportunity to hear a discussion about "death and deathlessness" that fascinated me.

Chapter 11: The Blue Ethers

"The root of all fears is the fear of death. Once you root out the supreme fear, all other fears lose their electricity."

—Jai Dev Singh, *Life Force Academy*

During Sat Nam Fest, I met Jai Dev Singh, a world-renowned teacher of Kundalini yoga and Ayurveda, an author, and the founder and principal teacher of the Life Force Academy, a global community for yogic teachings in over 60 countries.

Figure 27 - Spiritualist Jai Dev at Sat Nam Fest 2019 - Photo by Katie Clark

He gave a dynamic workshop on deathlessness during which he spoke about the five blue ethers, which are the stages through which one passes after one leaves this world and enters the hereafter. This immediately caught my attention, because several of the stages were consistent with my experiences in The Place Between Here and There.

After Jai Dev's workshop, I spent a great deal of time meditating on the five blue ethers and not only were they consistent with my experience, but they helped me understand my place within them and provided more depth and mind-blowing moments about the beauty of life and death. The more I thought about the five blue ethers, the more I began to realize that, perhaps, I was either misinterpreting some of the things that I had experienced, or that they added a deeper understanding of my experiences. This also helped me to not feel alone, and to realize that other people had these experiences as well.

The first blue ether is the stage in which the individual's experiences are synced with the Akashic record. The Akashic record is a compendium of all human events, thoughts, words, emotions, and intentions ever to have occurred in the past, present, or future.

This record holds not only all of the lifetimes of the individuals and how their actions were felt by themselves and others, but also how global events were shaped by group consciousness. This is akin to what other NDE (near-death experience) experiencers have described as their lives flashing before their eyes and their experiencing all of their life in an instant.

At first glance, this seemed implausible. How could every single action of your consciousness, another's consciousness and the group consciousness, be shared? That would be an impossibly vast amount of information, which would not seem to be necessary or purposeful. Would it really be necessary to know why Aunt Rose painted her bathroom pink, or why Cousin Billy chose to play baseball when he was actually better at soccer? Would it be necessary to know every political decision made by every country since the beginning of time?

When I think of my first experience in The Place Between Here and There, or what would be termed the first blue ether, I felt that I learned "the language of the Universe," and I was taught about spirituality and the connected nature of all of us, which had nothing to do with syncing up to the Akashic record.

After meditating on it for a while, I began to realize that syncing to the Akashic record was exactly what had really happened. It was not that I was receiving all of the minutiae of the Universe. I was receiving the knowledge of the Universe – not every single and mundane factor that created this knowledge, but the knowledge itself. I did not experience everyone's unique experiences, but how they felt about their experiences and what conclusions they drew from their experiences. Likewise, that is what I shared with the Universe. Basically, I downloaded the wisdom of the Universe, and I shared my wisdom with the Universe.

This is consistent with me meeting my higher self for the first time. I could see the beauty in my higher self. I could see the self-realization, the happiness, and the bliss in my higher self, being a divine and perfect higher version of me. I could also see all the lessons that my higher self learned in order to achieve this divine state, but I could not see the actual circumstances or events that caused this state of being.

I knew that very sad things happened, and that very happy things happened, but I knew that my higher self was content with all the experiences and felt that they were all beautiful as they resulted in necessary soul growth and divine enlightenment. This is what I think is reflected in the Akashic record. It must be the wisdom of the Universe.

While meditating on this new awareness that I gained from pondering the first blue ether, I began to wonder what exactly is the Akashic record? Is it a vault, like a pirate's treasure chest, that for some reason unbeknownst to us, is maintained, or is the Akashic record the consciousness of the creator, and we are part of that consciousness? Do our collective consciousnesses form the consciousness of the creator? Is that our purpose here? Is that what we add to the creator and the creation – our experiences, our understandings, and our spiritual growth? Is that the purpose of our existence? Is the creator perfect, or does the creator learn and grow with our experiences and that is the purpose of us and our experiences, and the Akashic record is part of that growth?

These are just questions that I do not have the answers to, but one thing of which I am now certain is that I did experience this first blue ether. I did receive the wisdom of the Universe, and I did share my wisdom with the Universe. It was much more than my first impression that I termed, "I learned the language of the Universe."

The second blue ether is where you review your life and determine whether there are any lessons which you have yet to learn from your life and whether you have completed all of the things which you were supposed to have completed in this incarnation.

After this life review, if it is certain that you have learned all of your intended lessons, you are tested on that knowledge to see whether you should be pulled into another incarnation at this time, proceed to the third blue ether in which you could become a spirit guide, or return to Earth in your current incarnation to finish learning the lessons you missed. This was very consistent with my experience. Therefore, to hear Jai Dev speak about this during the workshop was validating and truly helped me to understand the process.

Within my experience, once I learned the language of the Universe, i.e., synced with the Akashic record, I reviewed my entire life – every moment, every second. It was not that I was reliving it, rather that I was feeling all of the feelings that I felt at the time, while also feeling everyone else's feelings at that time as well. A lot of these feelings were elusive to me during my life, but I was truly feeling them during this review.

There were two differences now, though. Number one was that since I had already experienced it all once, that brought a certain insight that I did not possess before. The second was that after syncing to the Akashic record and knowing the wisdom of the Universe, I was able to experience a deeper spiritual understanding of each action and each event.

After reviewing my entire life once, I learned new lessons from my experiences and from my understanding of the Universe, and I grew spiritually as well. With this new understanding, I reviewed my life again. This process repeated again and again. With each life review, I grew more spiritually, and I was prepared to look at my life yet again with that increased spirituality. I was then able to draw new lessons from my experiences which raised my awareness and my spirituality even more.

This happened over and over and over again. I could not put a number to how many times it happened, but it was closer to infinity than it was to one. I was not choosing to review it, it just happened. It was as if the need drove the process, as opposed to a conscious decision on my part. As long as I kept learning from my past experiences, I kept reviewing my life over and over again, until I eventually stopped learning and I had no unfinished lessons from my past incarnation here on Earth. Once again, this is consistent with the description of the second blue ether. This virtual fine-tuning process is essential before one moves on to the next blue ether.

For me, the first blue ether, which was the syncing to the Akashic record, and the first half of the second blue ether, which was the life review and fine-tuning process, was what I experienced in the work-like setting in The Place Between Here and There.

The second part of the second blue ether, in which I was tested on my knowledge of the lessons learned, is what I experienced in the neighborhood bar and grill setting. It was in that bar and grill that I was put in charge of the children, who I later learned were spirits who were yet to have a human experience. I thought I was there to teach these children simple tasks at the bar and grill, but I was really there to prepare them for their upcoming Earthly existence.

I was being tested to see if I had learned all that I could from my life review and go on to become a spirit guide in the next blue ether.

This is the test I failed. I was unable to use the lessons that I had learned in the first part of the second blue ether to prepare the children for their new incarnations. They just would not listen to me, accept my guidance, or see me as a mentor. They merely saw me as someone with whom they had to be bothered. I failed to see their spirits. I failed to see their connected nature. I failed to see them as anything but young adults learning how to work in a bar and grill.

This really is a big lesson, because this is what life – physical incarnation – is about. You see people playing a certain role, doing an activity, in a circumstance, which really has nothing to do with the reason why they are there. There is deeper meaning in everything, and the ability to see this is essential for progressing into the third blue ether.

I am still questioning the presence of Kathie's higher self in the second blue ether. It was obvious that the kids were very disturbed by her presence. It was also obvious that when in this "test" setting of the second blue ether, no other soul is there if they do not have a purpose. This makes me wonder – was Kathie's higher self there in this place to ensure that I came back to Earth? Was she the reason I failed the test and had to come back? Did she know that we had a purpose together in life and that somehow my accident came in the way of that soul mission? These are things that I do not truly know, but I do know that I failed my test, and I do know that Kathie had something to do with it.

We are together, here and now on Earth, sharing this experience with a higher purpose in life, and perhaps our higher selves were waiting for this moment all along. Kathie was always telling me that I should speak of my experience and share it with the world. Maybe that is why her higher self was there – to make sure I came back to do that because I almost made it to the third blue ether.

In the third blue ether, one becomes a spirit guide, or in the Christian sense an angel, to provide assistance and guidance to spirits on Earth. Since I was unable to prove that I was able to be a spirit guide, after being tested in the second blue ether, I was returned to my human incarnation and did not proceed to the third blue ether. I had failed the test, because I could not get the children at the bar and grill to learn from me. Apparently, I did not gain enough insight and awareness after my life reviews.

It was not until my higher self touched my shoulder and downloaded his wisdom into me that I realized the true circumstances. I needed to come back to this current Earthly incarnation because I had yet to finish my soul mission. My friends, John and Joey, were in this third blue ether, which was why they were able to be spirit guides to me. I am glad they passed their tests.

The fourth blue ether, which I did not experience as I was not evolved enough to go there, is where a spirit goes when it is not going to be incarnated again. It is here that one finds the residences of the ascended masters, individuals who have lived in physical bodies, acquired the wisdom and mastery needed to become free of the cycles of re-incarnation and karma, and have attained their "ascension."

Ascension is merging with your higher self. These are beings such as Jesus, Buddha, Kuan Yin, Ghandi, and Saint Germain, to name a few. It is in this blue ether where the spirit understands the consciousness of the creator, the will of the creator, and the purpose of the Universe.

Finally, the fifth blue ether is where one is at one with the consciousness of the creator – their consciousness and the creator's consciousness are one. It is here that we merge with All That Is. This is where we become one with the Universe. Once an ascended being enters this ether, he or she will never return to another ether or incarnation.

I still somewhat struggle with the concept of the five blue ethers, because the more I meditate on them, the more questions I have. First off, there is not a lot of information, at least in western literature, or in reference material, to learn more about them. If this material was available, I would want to see if any other events which may have happened to me during my experience in The Place Between Here and There that seemed immaterial or inconsequential at the time, but that now, with a deeper understanding associated with the blue ethers, were actually more meaningful.

Secondly, what are the origins of the five blue ethers? If they are about the death process, how would somebody know about these things? If they did know about these things, they would be dead. Did we receive it from a yogi meditating on a mountain? Was it achieved through the meditations of a spiritual master? Was it evolved through millennia of warfare, with so many people being injured, that one in a million soldiers had a near-death experience, during which time they were provided with the knowledge of the five blue ethers, and then came back and recounted the same story? I do not know. Although, I would want to know that. I would want to know how real this is, because it does fit very well with my experience in The Place Between Here and There.

A significant thing that I learned from Kathie was that all of the messages and synchronicities that I was experiencing after the death of my son were not coincidences, even though I stubbornly adhered to the idea that they were initially. It was not until I was confronted with unquestionable evidence of these occurrences that I finally accepted them. Is this the same circumstance? Is the similarity of my experience with the five blue ethers a coincidence or are they indeed real? I have almost enough evidence to believe that they are real.

This also brings another question to my mind. If this process of the five blue ethers is what occurs after someone has passed, and I had not passed, why was I there? For an extended period of time - for several weeks - I was teetering on the verge of life and death, and the doctors were doubtful that I would survive. The only reason I was surviving was because I had access to some of the most advanced medical technology in one of the premier trauma centers in the world. So very few people on Earth have access to this level of medical care, now or ever. So, this brings up many thoughts.

Why did this happen, if I was not dead? What I am thinking is that this is an automatic process. This is not initiated by some consciousness beyond myself which says that this person is ready to take these steps and that they have officially died and are ready. Jai Dev referred to these auto-processes at the time of the body's transitioning as "life force intelligence."

I believe this is linked to your physical body in the same way that the sun shines and gravity works. It is a physical process which was manipulated by advanced medical technology. In any other time in the human existence, I was dead. But because those machines were keeping me alive, I was alive. I do think that as time goes on and as medical technology advances even more, there will be more and more recollections about The Place Between Here and There, because technology will enable more and more people to be in both the physical state and the spiritual state at the same time.

Chapter 12: Signs, Signs, Everywhere a Sign

"The Universe conspires to reveal the truth and to make your path easy if you have the courage to follow the signs."

—Lisa Unger, *Beautiful Lies*

While this is a hard concept to grasp, regardless of your level of spiritual awareness or enlightenment, the truth is that the Universe is always communicating with us. However, we are so caught up in our physical existence that we tend to be blind to the signs, synchronicities and obvious communications coming from the spirit realms and from the divine workings of the Universe.

The Universe will line up opportunities for your soul growth, as it wants you to succeed, expand, and achieve your highest state of consciousness, by using its own language of symbols. These symbols come in the way of meetings with the right people, synchronistic opportunities, appearances of angel numbers, correct gut instincts and intuitions, prophetic dreams, and more. As you validate these signs and synchronicities, believe in them, and express gratitude for them, more signs come your way.

This is also true regarding communication with those that have crossed over into spirit. Your loved ones may pass into another realm, but they still want you to succeed along your highest spiritual path and will communicate to you in this same way. By keeping your faith and belief, also known as staying in your highest vibration, you are open to this communication. When you do open your mind to the reality of this universal language, you will be keener to see it all around you. It is always at work, for your highest good.

To understand this, you must believe and know that these signs and synchronicities have a purpose, and not just think, "Oh wow I got a message from Uncle Tony." In many ways, that validates that communication is possible, and that validation is cool. But, moreover, the Universe, in fact, gives you guidance, and the way you understand this guidance and see this guidance will demonstrate if you are on the right path or not.

If you see a sign and you recognize it as such, and you take the advice the sign is giving you, you will see another sign, and yet another sign. The more you walk the path that the Universe sees as your destiny, the more signs you will receive. So, looking for signs just to know that your lost loved one is communicating may bring you peace, but to really get the true value, you need to understand the message. There is a dual meaning - the fact that they are communicating, and the important message. The more you hear and heed that message, the more messages you will see.

After my son Nick passed, roses were being presented to me repeatedly during the week of his death anniversary. I did not recognize or validate them as signs, even though Kathie strongly insisted that they were. Even when the psychic validated it during my cousin Lisa's visit, by saying Nick had a synchronicity with Saint Therese and was sending the roses, I still dismissed the signs.

It was not until Kathie read the Saint Therese biography card to me, which proved that Nick and Saint Therese had the synchronicities with the shared date of birth, and his passing on her canonization day, that I then saw these signs were connected and were, in fact, very real. The Universe was speaking to me. I finally understood that, and once I did, I began to see and recognize more signs and realize the synchronicities.

When I was with Kathie in Caumsett State Park and we came upon a large broken heart made of shells, in a remote and far away location, I took that as a sign that the Universe wanted us to mend our broken hearts. When Kathie found that all the shells needed to repair the heart were within reach, while the remainder of the beach contained none of these types of shells at all, I took that as a sign that Kathie and I had all that we needed within reach to start the next chapter of our lives together and become a couple. I asked the Universe for another sign because I was not sure how the people in our lives would take this information. Would we be accepted as a couple by them?

That sign was presented while Kathie and I took a walk again in Caumsett State Park, and on the very spot where we earlier found the broken heart which we mended, stood a dozen roses. I took that to mean that we should proceed with a new life together and that Nick was saying it was okay, because he sent roses, again. We have since found roses on several occasions when speaking of Nick, and they have become our symbol from spirit regarding Nick, just like silver hearts are the way Kathie's brother communicates with her.

Both Kathie and I have experienced more signs and synchronicities than we can put into words. It is truly remarkable. The most recent one occurred when Kathie and I were taking a morning walk on the beach, as we always do. On this particular day, Kathie was doing a walking meditation, and I was listening to a podcast. After we walked a few miles, we began talking. Kathie was telling me that she was doing a violet flame meditation and that she was sending the healing rays of the violet flame to the Earth. We were in the beginning of the Covid-19 pandemic, and she wanted to heal the world. She then told me that she asked Saint Germain, the ascended master that brings forth the violet flame, for a sign that he had heard her. Together, we looked for a sign, assuming it would be violet-colored beach glass, to no avail.

Then, we came upon a woman with an adorable dalmatian puppy. During a short chat at a reasonable distance, Kathie asked the woman the name of her dog. Lo and behold, she responded, "Violett." We both gasped, because what would be the odds of asking for a sign of the violet flame and meeting a dog named Violett? Kathie did want a nice piece of violet beach glass, but she was just as thrilled that she received the validation from a pup, a more unlikely source.

We departed ways with the woman. Later that day, I told Kathie that we should have gotten her phone number, because I just got this gnawing feeling that this was a connection that we should have followed up on. The Universe placed a woman with a dog named Violett in our path, which could not be happenstance. I knew this was purposeful. We were meant to connect with this woman.

This synchronicity felt like a universal pull, so each day, we looked for her again, to no avail.

A month went by and we had not seen the woman or her dog. One day, while Kathie was walking by herself, she was reciting violet flame decrees, which are mantras that call forth the violet flame healing energy. No coincidence here – the woman once again appeared with Violett. This time Kathie approached the woman, due to my insistence that there was a connection needing to be made, and she told her about how her dog's name was a validation that she had asked for from Saint Germain. Although Kathie was afraid that the woman would think she was crazy, it turned out that the woman was very receptive to the conversation.

Figure 28 - Voilett and Jeannine Tayler- Stack at Sunken Meadow Park

She went on to explain that "coincidentally," her dog was named Violett, because her son had also passed in an accident and he sends her violet-colored signs from Heaven. She also went on to say that her other son is about to get his wings from the Air Force, and "coincidentally," it turns out that the day of the ceremony is the same day as her recently transitioned son's birthday. Kathie and the woman agreed that these are definitely synchronicities, not coincidences.

The woman, who we now know as Jeannine Tayler- Stack, is a firm believer in signs and synchronicities as well, and she and Kathie became friends. The synchronicities with the dog Violett, the fact that she lost her son and that I lost my son, and that Kathie and Jeannine are both high vibrational spiritual beings, who also enjoy hiking, yoga, and fitness, meant that this meeting was supposed to happen. There were conversations that needed to be had between us, and the Universe brought us together to ensure that it would happen. I am sure this connection will produce more synchronicities going forward, and I am excited to see where they lead.

What is worth mentioning here is that sometimes the sign you seek is not the sign you get. While Kathie asked for violet beach glass, she instead got a dog named Violett. One could easily dismiss that sign, because it was not the exact sign for which she asked. You must realize that sometimes the Universe gives you a sign that is similar to what you asked for, but not exact. You need to keep an open mind and not be blind to the obvious nature of the communication.

The Universe can be playful in its use of signs. Kathie's daughter Kristen is a very grounded individual. She loves nature and hiking in the woods and on the beach. She talks to the animals and truly feels a deep connection with all of creation. Kristen is also quite spiritually connected, and very well-balanced. Her boyfriend Sean is an amazing athlete and a talented musician, but more amazing is his ability to meditate and connect with his higher self and the higher dimensions of consciousness. He was not inherently a nature lover and spent zero time hiking anywhere. Therefore, Kristen's ongoing pleadings with him to get out in nature with her were rather fruitless. This lack of nature caused Sean to sometimes be ungrounded, and while he was fully aware of this, he still had no desire to venture outdoors.

One day, Kristen coerced Sean to take a walk on the beach. Between Sean's episodes of moaning, he was able to spot some beautiful and extremely rare pieces of beach glass, which kept him quite interested in the walk. Knowing Kathie is a big fan of beach glass, Sean was excited to show her his finds.

Figure 29 - Kristen and Sean resting from beach glass hunting

To Kathie's shock and surprise, Sean produced a large, red marble, a rather coveted piece in the beach glass world. To Kristen's shock and surprise, Sean declared that he really enjoyed looking for beach glass and wanted to walk again the next day. Amazingly, Sean found another beautiful piece of red beach glass that day. A few days later, Sean found yet a third exotic piece of red beach glass. Despite being extremely jealous of Sean's "luck" in finding this glass, Kathie was happy that Sean was walking with Kristen and bringing her joy. Most important, though, Kathie was happy that Sean was enjoying the grounding aspects of walking in nature.

The moment of Sean's awakening occurred shortly thereafter when he exclaimed, "Hey Ma, do you think the Universe is sending me red beach glass to let me know that I need to start grounding in nature more?" Of course, Kathie emphatically stated yes, and I pointed out that since red is the color of the root chakra, the chakra which provides grounding, these were two signs being presented to Sean. Sean is now grounding in nature every day, and Kristen is now thrilled to have an avid hiker, beach glass hunter, and an aspiring tree-hugger as her boyfriend.

Kathie and I receive spirit communications which relate to our faith. Conversely, a Hindu that asks for signs might receive communications from Krishna or Ganesha, and a Buddhist that asks for signs might receive communications from Maitreya or Mahakala. As we are all one and there really is no chosen religion, we are really receiving these communications from the Universe or the All That is.

Once you validate and see the signs, you receive more. The signs are literal – signs from the Universe. They are like the signposts on a road. The synchronicities are the path. You observe the signs, and they each take you down your synchronistic path. This is the language of the Universe. It will guide you on your path, via the signs and synchronicities.

Chapter 13: Back to the Here and Now

"You can't go back and change the beginning, but you can start where you are and change the ending."

—C. S. Lewis

It has been five years since Steve went to The Place Between Here and There, four years since Nick passed away, and one year since Steve regained almost all of his physical strength and mental capacity. Since that time, so much has happened that it could encompass an entire new book. To be succinct, let us just say that we have grown so much as individuals, as a couple, and as a part of the collective consciousness of the Universe. This growth was somewhat of a forced expeditious growth, since unplanned events led to this life-changing journey, but it was all worth it. There was so much pain, but so much glory, and one needs that contrast to appreciate the difference.

Figure 30 - Ananda, Fort Salonga, Long Island

We presently live in a cute little house one town over from Kings Park. It is an exact and amazing manifestation of our dreams. We wanted a home within walking distance to the water, and we wanted to decorate it with beach décor and crystals. Well, I wanted to decorate it with beach décor and crystals, and, after Steve's many attempts to hang up Harley Davidson pictures and items that were not cohesive with the home's original color scheme failed, he learned to want to decorate the house with beach décor and crystals. See, he was growing as a spirit after all.

Figure 31 - The Zen of It All, Kathie and Steve's Ananda interior

Steve even went far and above what I even dreamed of and helped turn the home into a Zen sanctuary, replete with statues of our favorite saints and angels, mantra music playing 24 hours a day, 7 days a week, jars of beach glass, trays of heart-shaped rocks, buckets of sea shells, shelves and shelves of crystals, and a healing room filled with gongs, Tibetan and crystal singing bowls, chimes and all manner of healing modality gadgets and gizmos.

The home, which we named Ananda, meaning bliss or happiness in Sanskrit, has been the host of many spiritual gatherings, full and new moon ceremonies, kirtans, group meditations, spiritual yoga practices, and more mainstream activities, like family parties and dinners with friends.

Steve still works in the computer industry, solving people's computer problems, although we now know that he is really solving more than computer problems. As occurred in The Place Between Here and There, Steve oftentimes finds himself mentoring young professionals just entering the workforce. In his capacity of Information Technology Project Manager, he hires entry-level employees, fresh out of college, and in "his way," teaches them more than they thought they would ever learn. When I say "his way," I would say that if you truly knew Steve, this would be plain and clear, but I will explain it for those that do not know him.

Steve is not only a knowledgeable computer professional that truly knows how to help others gain technical expertise, as well as communication skills, business savvy, and the discernment necessary to succeed in their jobs, but he also has "this way" of connecting on a soul level. In short time, Steve always becomes a guru of spiritual awareness and helps others see and seek the meaning behind the meaning of life. He just has a way of bringing people to new levels of spiritual enlightenment which helps them succeed in all areas of their lives. As a result of Steve's trip to the second blue ether, in which he failed the test of providing guidance to the kids, I believe that it is his task now on Earth. Hopefully, he will pass this test. I think he might!

I am working in childcare, as I retired from a corporate America job years ago, and I enjoy watching and assisting in the growth of little souls that enter this Earth plane. They definitely seem to be incarnating with much more spiritual awareness nowadays and will hopefully help usher us into the age of enlightened mass consciousness soon.

I was also recently working in elder care, assisting a beautiful 86-year old soul transition from Earth life to her original heavenly home. This amazing lady, Eleanor, needed to be placed into a facility due to acquiring Alzheimer's later in life and her need for constant monitoring. I was hired as her part-time aide. At first, I thought I was there to help her, but little did I know that she was actually there to help me.

Figure 32 - Eleanor with her daughters, Susan on left, and Eileen on right
Photograph courtesy of Susan Alexander

As I reported for work each morning, I tended to Eleanor and enjoyed our time together. In a short time, we became close friends. She did not possess a short-term memory and asked me a hundred times per day what I was doing that day or what I ate for breakfast, but her long-term memory was sharp as a tack.

Eleanor could describe in detail every aspect of her life, and it was a beautiful one. She continually provided sage advice for my little life crises, as well as glorious stories of a life well lived, a love well lived, and a bond with her children and their families well lived. It was immediately apparent that Eleanor was the happiest person in the nursing home, which her daughters and I named "The Club," so that Eleanor could feel that she was still hanging out at her family's exclusive beach resort, rather than a nursing home.

As I witnessed Eleanor joyously loving every day at the club, while others continually were depressed, crying, and sad, I came to the realization that it is very important that we live like Eleanor did – full of positivity, full of grace, full of gratitude, and full of love – because when our physical minds start to deteriorate, and our short-term memories disappear, our soul's essence, the memories that get stored into our "Akashic records" are what remain. While on Earth, we need to focus on building beautiful memories, like Eleanor did, because they are critical to our ascension process in the blue ethers.

I saw Eleanor the day before she took her last breath. I knew she had no fear of death, because she already knew of the continuation of consciousness. We spoke of these things often. I was so happy to know she would be reuniting with her soulmate and releasing the pains of the physical body, although I knew her loving family, and I, would miss her so much. But I am so grateful I got to know her at all, for she was a valuable guru.

Eleanor made a choice every day to be joyful, to be grateful, and to give and receive love. It is for that reason that I know that she did not even need a test in the second blue ether. She went right to the third blue ether, and she is a spiritual guide to us on Earth.

I can sense her presence at times, as she had this sassy way of pointing out my silly mistakes and horrible fashion sense, as she was one classy lady with impeccable taste in clothing. I can sense her hearty laugh and see her warm smile, in my mind's eye, as she imparts her wise and much-needed advice. After Eleanor's passing, I never returned to a job in elder care. I know I was there to learn what I needed to learn, and it was only through my connection with Eleanor that it would happen.

Every morning before work, Steve and I walk at the local beach or the nearby hiking trails with our pups. It is as if we are living a dream - being able to walk and talk, while grounding and feeling the connection that we innately have to nature, while also relishing in the fact that every moment we share is sacred. We are beyond grateful that we feel and understand the importance of and reverence for nature and All That Is, for that truly is the greatest and most needed happy pill on Earth.

Coming full circle, it is not coincidental that our walks on our favorite local beach begin with eastward sunrise strolls, denoting a new beginning each day to be better, to grow more, and to shine our light in the world. The real synchronicity, however, is that in the eastern sky, right on the horizon, at first light, is the silhouette of Stony Brook University Hospital, the wonderful institution that saved

Steve's physical life. There is not a morning that we do not see and feel grateful for that hospital, for that moment in time, and for everything that has happened since that moment in time. We will never take moments for granted again.

Figure 33 - Sunrise walk at Callahan's Beach, Northport, with Stony Brook Hospital on the distant right, just under the rising sun.

Steve and I would love to open a spiritual center one day and continue our workshops. We are presently involved in various trainings, like spiritual yoga, Reiki, energy work, and sound healing. I even coerced Steve into attending a crystal certification class. Steve pretends that he does these things to pacify me. However, if you saw him in the classes, you would notice immediately that he is the one who participates the most, sits in the front row, center seat, asks questions, volunteers information, offers to set up, clean up, stay late, and so on and so on. Oh right... he does that for me...

Steve laughs when he says that if the guy he was ten years ago met the guy he is today, he would beat the crap out of him. The guy who once donned black Harley Davidson clothing, listened to heavy metal music, and frequented bars and biker establishments, was now wearing white, going to yoga, exclusively listening to ancient mantra music in

Sanskrit, and replaced his carnivore diet with tofu, bean burgers, and vegan cheeses. What a radical difference.

Figure 34 - The transmuted Steve at Sat Nam Fest

Steve and I plan on hosting more workshops on The Place Between Here and There, and writing more books. It is our sincerest desire to help others heal their grief by understanding the continuation of consciousness and our connection to one another and spirit, to understand the meaning of life by knowing that all experiences are opportunities for spiritual growth on a soul level, and to use higher awareness to achieve bliss while here on Earth.

Epilogue

While in the coma, communication with my friend Kathie was pivotal in my life and helped me truly understand my experience in The Place Between Here and There and the connectivity of all souls. There are souls in this life that are meant to be with you for either a brief moment, in order to help you learn a lesson, or a lifetime, to help you experience continual soul growth. Kathie was obviously meant to share life with me and to grow with me. Then, there was another person, Barbara Williams, who was meant to come into my life briefly to assist me during the most crucial time in my life, when I was on the brink of life and death.

At the time, I did not know she was there for me, and she did not know the impact it would have on me, but that is the beauty of life. There is an interconnection between souls that is so beneficial and so beautiful, whether it is apparent or just under the surface. Barbara was under the surface, but what she did and what it meant to me was beautiful and necessary for my soul.

Barbara Williams was Sean's hockey skating coach. Barbara was a local legend due to her prestigious past working with many famous National Hockey League (NHL) players, in addition to her reputation as being a tough coach whose commanding demeanor made men out of boys. She was in great demand from the parents whose young sons dreamed of making the big time.

Sean was certainly lucky to have gained a weekly appointment in Barbara's busy schedule. This amazing woman was very important in my life as well, although for reasons other than hockey, as neither of my kids even played hockey.

In addition to being the songwriter and guitarist for our Between Here and There workshops, as well as Kathie's daughter's boyfriend, Sean Reilly is an aspiring pro hockey player, as well as an aspiring singer/songwriter, with dreams of playing for an NHL franchise in the not-too-distant future. When Sean was talking to me one day about his practice and mentioned Barbara's full name, a light went off in my head. "What a coincidence," I told Sean, "I know Barbara. What a small world."

Figure 35 - Stephen Mundinger, Barbara Williams and Sean Reilly
Photograph courtesy of Barbara Williams

I told Sean that I sat in the stands with Barbara, watching a sporting event, while she told me all about her life. She explained how she was hired as a skating coach to teach professional hockey players how to improve their skating ability. Up until that time, most of the coaching was centered on the strategy of playing the game, not necessarily on skating. Barbara was convinced that if the players could skate better, they could be better hockey players.

Barbara was quite proud of her time coaching the likes of Mark Messier and other popular hockey hall-of-famers. It was hard not to be completely in awe of this woman. As an advocate for strong women, since I had a daughter that I was raising to be a strong woman, I loved hearing Barbara's inspirational story.

I remember getting a message from Barbara a couple of years ago, saying that her son had passed away and that she was heartbroken. She wanted to talk to me. I had lost my son Nick a year earlier, so I understood why she was reaching out to me. I understood what she must be going through, as we were both part of that club that no one wants to be a part of - the parents who lost their child club.

I wrote back to her, expressing my heartfelt sympathies, and I recounted our long conversations. I told her that although I remembered our talks quite well, for the life of me, I just could not remember which sporting event we attended when we spoke. I never heard back from her.

I had wanted to speak to Barbara about her son. Therefore, when I heard that she was Sean's coach, I asked him to invite her to our upcoming workshop. As we learned from the many letters, emails, and texts we received afterwards, The Place Between Here and There Workshops often helped grieving people to feel better, so I thought it would be a good opportunity for Barbara and me to finally connect and speak about our sons.

About a day before the workshop, I got a phone call from a woman asking, "Hello, is this Steve Weber?" I remembered that voice well and replied, "Yes, is this Barbara Williams?" She replied that it was and asked, "How did you know it was me?" I told her that I recognized her voice and that I remembered our long discussions about her time as a skating coach for the NHL. I also told her about my puzzlement regarding when these discussions took place, since I could remember all the details, especially sitting in the bleachers together, but I just could not remember where or even which sporting event that we were watching.

To my astonishment, Barbara said that we never sat on the bleachers together. She said that her son was in the hospital when I was in the coma. He was in the very next room. For 14 days, each day after she visited with her son, Barbara would come into my room, sit with me, and hold my hand. She would whisper the Lord's Prayer in my ear and tell me all about her life.

Barbara knew of me from my involvement in the town, and this tough-as-nails woman graciously and kindly gave her time to speak to me while I was in the coma. Like Kathie, she knew communication was possible during the in-between stage of life and death, and I heard and appreciated every word that she said.

An Important Note About Kundalini Yoga

It is very important that we make mention of some recent and unsettling developments in the Kundalini yoga community. A book recently came out which made serious allegations of abuse against the yogi that brought Kundalini yoga to America, Yogi Bjahan.

As a society, we have been awakened to the realities of the damages caused by abuse. We know the horrors of the abuse and the life-long trauma felt by the victims. We know that no one is truly safe – not girls, not boys, not women, not men – no one. We know that we must be vigilant and aware, and we now know that we can speak up without fear of shame or retribution.

Kundalini yoga is an ancient practice of over 5,000 years. It is deeply connected with the spiritual customs and practices of India, and it is not connected to any one person or any one religion. Kundalini Yoga is a spiritual practice that is shared by all of humanity and elevates consciousness. Kundalini yoga has become a great passion of ours, and Steve and I practice at least once a day. The benefits of a yoga practice are numerous, and yoga has been instrumental to us physically, emotionally, and spiritually.

In addition to attending yoga classes at Kundalini Yoga Long Island, we have also been practicing yoga with the most loving and compassionate teacher, Tina Marie Bertoli, at Family Tree Yoga in Nesconset, New York. The fact that her classes are always at maximum capacity is undeniable proof of her ability to profoundly impact the lives of others, and she certainly has had a profound impact on ours. Her practice encompasses a channeling of angelic and divine wisdom that helps her students learn how to navigate through the challenges of life, and it also includes a physical practice that is wonderful for strength and fitness.

Although Tina teaches this ancient form of yoga, she does so with her own unique flair and talent which leaves everyone feeling high and blissful after each class. Most importantly, Tina always instructs us to connect to the teacher within, which is our higher self, not to emulate or worship another person.

Figure 36 - Kathie, Tina Marie Bertoli, and Steve at Family Tree Yoga in Nesconset, New York – Photograph courtesy of Joe Daniele, Cineshooter Inc.

Of course, we understand what that means, since that was an important lesson we learned from Steve's experience in The Place Between Here and There – that our divine infinite spirit is our most important teacher. We are our own guru.

We hope that others learn to find a spiritual practice, either through yoga, meditation, music, walking the beach, or any other method that resonates with them.

There are many ways one can connect to their higher self and find bliss in this world. This world is a beautiful place, even when bad things happen, and the best way one can find that beauty is to look for it – it is everywhere.

Appendix 1:
Questions and Answers

How were you able to forgive the person who caused the death of your son, because if that happened to my son, I would never be able to do that?

Honestly, I feel that my visit to The Place Between Here and There is the only reason why I was able to forgive the person that contributed to the death of my son. Had I not learned those valuable lessons that I did while I was there, I am positive that I would be a hateful, and perhaps vengeful, wreck. However, after my life review, and after seeing the meaning behind all of the experiences we have on Earth, I learned that the young man who gave my son the bad drugs was also a soul, on a spiritual path, who experienced hardships and challenges in life that brought him to the state that made him become a drug dealer. Therefore, I did not wish any more pain and suffering upon him. What I did wish was that he would be able to become aware of how his actions affected not only my son, but all the others that became addicted or overdosed as a result of his actions.

Through this awareness, I wish that he would then be able to make something of his life and go on to do good in this world. I wish that he would become a good father, who would bring his son to football and wrestling, to band practice, to communion, and see him graduate college, get married, and have kids. That would bring me peace and closure – for him to become a good person who becomes a productive member of society, rather than one who continues on a path of devastation and destruction. It benefits no one to hold animosity against anyone, because we are all a collective consciousness, and holding animosity toward another is akin to holding animosity towards ourselves and towards the collective. Instead, if we forgive others, wish them well, offer them prayers, and shower them in light, we can change the world. The ripple effects caused by good people outweigh the ripple effects caused by bad people.

Did you have any residual issues resulting from your brain injury?

When I first woke up in the hospital, it was difficult for me to get my thoughts together. It could have been the drugs, because I was heavily sedated for a long time, but I felt like my brain was just working slow. I really had to think about every word I said. I knew I suffered a traumatic brain injury, but it felt like part of me was missing from my consciousness. I could remember the things that had happened in my life, but I could not remember how I felt about those things. It was as if my mind was deprogrammed from its reactions.

I do not know the medical term for this, but I would say that my reactive mind was erased. The reactive mind contains how you feel about your experiences, which is imprinted when the experiences occur. It seemed like that part of my brain is the part that was erased. It is perhaps one of the most primitive parts of your brain. It enables you to react quickly to events taking place in your life, without having to re-think them every time.

The memories of what had happened to me were all there, but how I felt about those memories was not there. This bothered me for a quite a bit, because not only did I not know if I would get my reactive mind back, but I wondered why I would have learned all of those valuable lessons and experiences in The Place Between Here and There if I was only going to come back and have to relearn those same lessons and experiences here.

Luckily, this was only a temporary situation. If I had to guess, I would say that my body was so severely injured that it needed as much internal power as necessary to heal, and that my brain had to forget certain things in order to relearn other things, like how to walk again, how to move muscles again, and how to use internal organs again.

There is only so much CPU and RAM in a human brain, and my brain needed to free up some resources in order to make room for all the processes necessary to heal. Perhaps my reactive mind was not necessary during the time it took for my physical body to rehabilitate. So, my physical body let that go in order to make room.

This brought my attention to an interesting parallel about what I learned about electro-shock therapy while working at the Kings Park Psychiatric Center. When the patients' minds were overloaded with information that was doing them harm, electro-shock treatments rebooted their minds so that they could erase their reactive minds and re-experience life in a more beneficial manner. The electro-shock therapy simulates a near-death experience, during which the body believes it suffered a traumatic injury, and erases the reactive mind, in order to make that brain power available to assist in the recovery process. I felt that my reactive mind was erased so that I could relearn to experience my life in a more beneficial manner.

My reactive mind and memories returned in a short period of time. As everything came back, I was able to re-examine my stored memories and make better sense of them all. Due to this experience, I now have a wonderful ability to view things from a neutral, rather than reactive, thought process, and can understand why things happen the way they do, and am able to and figure out the lessons I am meant to learn from them.

I feel it would be beneficial for others on the Earth plane to find some form of meditation or yoga practice in which they can learn to operate more in the neutral mind and consciously review their lives in this manner. It would lead to a more blissful existence and a greater opportunity for spiritual growth.

Most often, how you feel about something occurs when it happened to you. For example, if a 7-year old is bitten by a dog, that 7-year old remembers that incident for his entire life, and he is frightened every time he sees a dog. The fear remains in his reactive mind. If, as an adult, he reevaluated that situation with an adult's mind, he may determine the difference between an aggressive dog and a friendly dog and act accordingly, as opposed to being frightened by all dogs. We all have memories such as these that are stored in our reactive minds, that cause distress, and impede our growth.

After I had my reactive mind erased, I had the opportunity to re-create how I felt about my experiences, with the benefit of being a 50-something year old man, and the benefit of having the wisdom that I learned in The Place Between Here and There, so my entire psyche was re-created with a more stable and positive perspective. Others can learn to do this also. Through constantly revisiting your experiences in life, your new awareness helps you learn to re-evaluate your reactions and gain a deeper awareness of the meaning of each life event. This awareness helps you achieve a more blissful state in life.

How did you travel in The Place Between Here and There?

In The Place Between Here and There, I did not travel to get anywhere. I did not walk, fly, or travel in any way. I did not have control over where I was going. I just was. I had control over what I was doing when I was there, but I did not wake up and say that I wanted to be in a particular setting. The scene in which I found myself was the focus of everything. Wherever I was, I learned the deeper meaning and eventually understood why I was there and what I needed to learn. In this place, which was truly a place of life review, every scene was like a live play in which I re-experienced my life, learned from my actions and inactions, and then learned what the true and deeper meanings were for each scenario. I went from setting to setting until I stopped learning.

How does the telepathic communication work in The Place Between Here and There?

There is no actual verbal communication or mind-to-mind science fiction type of transferring of information. It is about awareness.   Everything there is about awareness. Awareness is the fundamental structure of all activity, communication, and learning in The Place Between Here and There. Inside of myself, I would be thinking about the need to know a bit of information. I would not be asking it of somebody else. I may be aware that someone else may know the answer, but if I am thinking about it, and it is part of my awareness, through the other spirit's awareness, they can sense my need to know this. If they have an answer or something that can help, I become aware of that part of their awareness.

When you said that "it was a beautiful place," what made it beautiful?

It was not that the sun was shining, and the birds were singing, and the mountains were majestic. It was not beautiful in the physical sense, because it was not a physical place. It was a place of the spirit. Imagine being in a place in which you were angry at nobody, were ashamed at nothing that you had done, loved everything and everything that had happened and All That Is loved you, where you had no anxiety, no fear, no pain, and nothing but bliss. Think about that. It is not that you were being shielded from these things. It is that you understood the meaning in all of it, and that brought you a sense of bliss. And, it was that sense of bliss that made it a beautiful place.

Other people who have had near death-experiences have described grand views of Heaven with amazing flowers, rolling green fields, and white marble learning halls, but I did not see any of that. Perhaps those scenarios were needed for those individuals to aid them after crossing over. I am not sure. I did not see the beautiful things other people described. Those things are related to the physical world, and although I was not a spiritual person, per se, I was a grateful person, who felt deep reverence for nature and life, and I often contemplated the meaning of life and the reasons why we are here.

Perhaps the nirvana-type setting was not necessary for my spiritual growth. Everyone's experience is different, based upon where they are in life when they passed. Take, for example, somebody who lived a very depressed or angry life. They would need to be held, coddled, and to see beautiful flowers, kind of like a happy dream, to get them into a more serene state before taking them to the next step of a life review, which could be quite shocking and surreal.

You said that you did not need to go to a beautiful place because you were grateful, had reverence and contemplated the meaning of life, but you were also a non-spiritual biker. This is very contrasting. Can you explain?

I would say that when I was a biker, I was not a biker in the true sense of the word. When it came to the skills of being a biker and looking the part, I fit the bill. I had been riding motorcycles since I was ten years old. I worked on my own motorcycle. I could tear the entire bike down to the crank in about an hour. But, when it came to the outlaw aspect of biking, that did not resonate with me at all. I was kind of like a sheep in wolf's clothing. You see, I came from a time period and an environment in which the "tough" guy was a predominant persona.

One is a product of one's environment. But, really, I was a sensitive individual – a deep thinker – that cared for others, cared for the animals, cared for the environment, and wanted to make a positive impact in the world. I did not subscribe to violence and combative behaviors often associated with outlaw bikers. Despite my troubled marriage, I was a happy guy because I was a biker. Being on a bike, traveling across states, for miles and miles, alone, is a form of meditation that is unsurpassed. I would ride through beautiful roads, open skies, watching sunrises and sunsets, and feel deeply grateful for my life, my breath, my opportunities, my health, my children, my friends, and my Harley.

On those long rides, I would contemplate the meaning of life, the purpose of existence, and if there was something more to just the five senses. The five senses are so alive on a motorcycle. I saw so many beautiful mountains, streams, and plains. I smelled so many pleasant aromas of flowers, the seas, and the grasses. I heard the rolling waters, the rumbling of the road, the singing of the birds, and the calling of the wild animals. I tasted the fresh air, the local food in each state, and I felt the sun on my face, and the wind in my hair.

With all of these experiences, I truly felt the wonder of the physical realm. It was alive in me, in every moment. After a awhile, the "oh wow" factor wears off, so you are left with only your own thoughts. It was during those times that I began to think about the Universe, and what there could be other than the five senses. Is this all that is? It was a meditation that went on for hours, days, weeks, months, and years.

On the outside, yes, I appeared to be a stereotypical outlaw biker, and that was how I felt comfortable appearing to the world. But, in myself, I was every bit a spiritualist. I just did not know that, because I had no one to talk to about it. That is one of the things that first attracted me to Kathie, because we were able to talk about these things. For the first time, I realized that I was not alone in these thoughts. She was an affirmation to me that other people thought these thoughts too. Therefore, when I went to The Place Between Here and There, I do not think I needed the rainbows and unicorns, because I already experienced them on Earth.

Do you feel that you are more evolved than other people now that you have had this experience?

I do not think that I am more evolved or less evolved than other beings. We are all on different paths, with the same destination, but we are at different levels of awareness. For any spiritual person to feel that they are "above" others is counter to the very essence of spirituality. All of our souls are connected, and no one part is greater than the whole.

We chose to come here together to experience individual, as well as group consciousness, and to lift each other up. A sign of a true enlightened human is compassion and love for all beings and the knowledge of our connectivity. Behind each pair of eyes that you see on this Earth, is a being that is part of God, the All That Is, the collective divine consciousness. We must put our egos aside and see the divinity of all beings. We are one.

Being that I had this experience, I became enlightened on so many levels, but I stayed the same on other levels. No one is perfect, regardless of their level of spiritual advancement. A guru, who is exalted for his esteemed spiritualty and put on a pedestal by many for that advanced enlightenment, might shock people when he displays physical flaws, like a short temper or an affinity for luxury. We must understand that we should not view any people as deities while they are here on Earth. Earth beings are all human and are evolved at different levels.

The Bible talks about giving up Earthly possessions as being a way into Heaven. How do you feel about that?

It is true that you cannot take anything physical with you when you pass. Your house, your car, your jewels, your clothing, your college degree, and your beauty remain as only memories in the Earth plane. The only things you take with you are your experiences. Therefore, what you have imprinted into your spirit is what is important. You will not benefit from having a luxury car, a safe full of gold bars, or having a lucrative job. You will, however, benefit from your good deeds, your compassionate words, your loving gestures, for rising in the face of challenges, and for seeking higher means of spiritual growth.

However, having beautiful Earthly possessions is not frowned upon. You are meant to live a life full of joy and abundance, and if that includes luxury, that is okay. You just need to know that acquiring these possessions is not the purpose of life. The purpose of life is experiencing soul growth, connecting to your higher consciousness, and understanding the connectivity of all living beings.

What are the chakras, and how can we balance them in order to live a better life?

The chakras are the energetic nerve centers in our body that correspond with different aspects of our psychological, emotional, and spiritual states of being. There are seven chakras. The first chakra, the root chakra, is located at the base of the spine and is the chakra of stability and security. It grounds us to the Earth and the physical existence. The second chakra, the sacral chakra, is located above the pubic bone and is the chakra of creativity and sexual energy.

The third chakra, the solar plexus chakra, is located just above the navel and is the chakra of personal power and courage. The fourth chakra, the heart chakra, is located around our heart center and is the chakra of all love, including self-love, compassion, and connection. This chakra is the bridge between our lower three chakras, which are physically based, and our upper three chakras, which are spiritually based.

The fifth chakra, the throat chakra, is in the area of the throat and is the chakra of communication, truth, and expression. The sixth chakra, the third-eye chakra, is located in between the eyebrows and is the chakra of intuition and inner awareness. The seventh chakra, the crown chakra, is located at the top of our head and is the chakra of enlightenment and spiritual connection to our higher selves and to the divine.

These chakras need to be balanced for us to have a positive human incarnation. If we are overloaded in one chakra or more than one, our system is off balance, and we will experience great challenges.

There are many ways you can balance your chakras, but I will discuss two that I know. The first way is to educate yourself on the chakras, which can be easily done online, and then use that knowledge to assess your own chakra weaknesses. For instance, if you have a lack of courage and confidence, you may have a weakness in your solar plexus chakra. If you are shy and find it hard to communicate, you may have a weakness in your throat chakra. Once your chakra weaknesses are identified, you can learn methods to balance them, through yoga, meditation, visualization, crystal placement, and more.

Another way to balance your chakras is to consult with a reiki or energy practitioner. They are trained to read the energy in your body and can actually manipulate your energy through various modalities, such as tuning forks, sound healing, reiki healing energy, crystal healing, and others.

Kathie and I are trained in reiki and crystal healing and use the above methods regularly. They have had a tremendously positive impact in our lives and the lives of others.

You have such a wealth of knowledge about life now. Are you a life coach or a mentor?

I am not a life coach or a mentor. I am just a guy who survived a near-fatal motorcycle accident. There are professionals in the health care industry who have doctorate degrees and decades of experience counseling people. There are spiritualists who spent their entire lives learning centuries old teachings on metaphysics. I have done neither of those. I am not qualified to counsel or teach, but due to my unique near-death experience, I gained valuable insight about the workings of the Universe and the meaning of life. Therefore, as a friend, I can listen to others and offer them advice on what I learned in The Place Between Here and There and can help them to examine their life experiences and possibly learn and grow from them. And so can you.

Kathie, can you describe the visitation you had from your mom after her passing?

My first visitation came while I was in a semi-awake state. I was resting on the couch after the funeral. My mom appeared to me in my kitchen and was walking toward the front door as if to leave. I screamed to her, "Mom, where are you going? I want to talk to you!" When she turned around, she had the appearance of being in her 30's, and she was the most glorious-looking being that I had ever seen. Her eyes were so clear and bright, and I could see tiny flecks of gold in them. It was apparent that those eyes contained all the wisdom of the Universe as well as all the love. She was an angelic soul, and her robes of gold shimmered like stardust. I was simply awestruck by her appearance. She was always a very beautiful woman, but now she was just dazzling and had a mesmerizing light emanating from her body.

Mom told me that she was glad that I called to her, because she could not come to me unless I asked her to. She then said that since she was summoned, I could ask any questions I wanted to, because she now had some time to talk with me. I immediately blurted out, "I love you, and I miss you so much. I cannot bear knowing I might not get to the place where you are when I pass. I need to be with you then. What do I have to do to get to the same place? Do I need to be a certain religion? Do I need to go to a certain church? Tell me how I can see you again." She calmly and reassuringly explained that we would always be together. She then said that there is no religion on the other side.

She told me that we are all one and that the reason that we come to Earth as spirits is to learn to do two things – to give love and to receive love. I was stunned. I challenged her and said, "What do you mean? That's it? Don't I need religion or faith?" Again, she said, "No, the Earth is a school that we come to in order to learn love. It is that simple. That is the meaning of life. And you need to tell others, especially your dad." She then said that she had to go but that she loved me and will see me again soon.

It was the most beautiful and comforting moment of my life. The peace I got from that visitation is what sustains me to this day. I knew, from my mom, that life is eternal and that I will always be connected to those that I loved.

Kathie had a visitation from her mom. Did you experience a visitation from Nick?

Yes, I did. I believe that when the spirit of the lost loved one finally adapts to their new reality and is moving on to the next step of spiritual development, they try to let you know that they are okay. When someone has this type of visit, it seems so real and leaves them feeling overwhelmingly peaceful. That is how you can tell the difference between a visitation dream and a regular dream.

During my visitation dream, Nick was with me in the form in which I last remembered him. However, he possessed a startling radiance now. His spirit was happy and light, which was counter to the last few years of his incarnation on Earth. I felt such a beautiful love and peace in him. The love emanating from his eyes showed me that whatever happened in his lifetime was meant to happen and that he was now enlightened and free from the chains of his physical existence. Before me stood an enlightened being, and that is all a father could want to see in his son.

When I awoke, I was still in that peaceful state. I realized it was just a dream; however, something was different about this dream that stuck with me. I just knew that everything was going to be alright, and I really felt that in my soul. For the first time since Nick's passing, the cloud of grief was lifted from me. And, for the first time, I could look at his pictures again, because up until that point I only felt sadness when I did.

I immediately called my mother and told her what had happened. I told her that Nick came to me in a dream to let me know that he was okay and that she could, once again, take out Nick's pictures and hang them on the wall. Like me, she was so grief stricken that she could not bear to look at his photographs either. I assured her that Nick was at peace, and we no longer needed to hang on to any grief. He did not want that at all.

I know that Nick left The Place Between Here and There and went on to either the third blue ether or back to an incarnation on Earth. So, I told mom to keep an eye out for Nick, just in case.

Kathie, you lost your twin brother quite young. Can you explain what happened?

Losing my twin brother, Tommy, was heart breaking. When you have a twin, you experience every aspect of life together, at precisely the same time - learning to walk and talk, attending schools, graduating, marrying, and trying to have kids. It creates such a tight bond. We truly loved one another.

As we grew older, our bond got stronger and stronger. We shared a love of playing sports and would spend hours a day playing tennis, golf, softball, or go biking, rollerblading, and ice skating. Even after we were both married, we spent several days a week playing tennis or going to batting and driving ranges. We also confided in each other and had no secrets. It was so wonderful having the type of relationship we had. Tommy was more of a best friend than a brother.

Figure 37 - Kathie's Mom Diane and Brother Tommy with Kathie circa 1990

Although we were similar in many ways, there was one difference, however, and that was that Tommy lived with an anxiety disorder, while I did not. This made many aspects of his life rather difficult, while my life was quite joyful. You would never know, in looking at Tommy, that this could be the case. He was massive – six feet, three inches tall, and 240 pounds of solid muscle. He was so athletic, so smart, and so funny. However, inside he felt anxiety every day. Therefore, he was on anti-anxiety medication, and this lasted for 20-something years.

The medication helped Tommy live a somewhat normal life, although he always had an inner saboteur that made his life harder than most. It hurt me that he lived like that. In my mind, he was so amazing, impressive, and wonderful, that he should not have had to feel that way. The doctor said Tommy's generalized anxiety disorder was caused by a chemical imbalance, so he just could not help but feel the way he did.

On the week preceding his accident, the doctor who filled his anti-anxiety medication prescription decided that Tommy had been on the drug too long and should immediately come off and start a different drug. It was a decision that would cost my brother his life. The minute my brother stopped taking the medication, he was in a fog. He was like a zombie. My dad and I were extremely frightened. My dad called the doctor to describe how debilitating the withdrawal was, but the doctor told him that Tommy would eventually feel better, so there was nothing to worry about. It was painful to see my beautiful twin looking so hollow and soul-less.

On the morning of the accident. Tommy was on the way to see my dad. He swerved off the road and went onto the shoulder. When he got out to walk and get help, he was hit by another car and killed. Had he been on the anti-anxiety medication which helped him function properly, this would not have happened. But he was not in a right state of mind, and I lost my only brother that day.

As difficult as it was to lose Tommy, I find peace in the fact that he does not have to live with anxiety any longer. I know he is in a beautiful place. I know he had a chance to review his life and learn why he had the challenges that he did. I know he experienced tremendous soul growth and now understands the continuation of consciousness and the fact that each consciousness is a part of the Creator. Therefore, he knows of his divinity. He did not know of it on Earth, but he knows it now. That makes me truly happy.

Like Nick, my brother was very physically imposing and quite strong in the lower chakras, while not very balanced in the upper chakras. I often wonder if Tommy and Nick both had more of a spiritual connection, could they have been spared some of the pain that they experienced in life? As a devout spiritualist, I can only imagine how destructive a lack of that connection would be for me. Therefore, wouldn't it be that way for others? We are spiritual beings living a human experience, and we need to be connected to both Heaven and Earth.

Western medicine tends to solely concentrate on pharmacology to treat illness. That is an important part of treatment, but I believe that they should not neglect spirituality and alternative healing modalities as well. If pharmacology is the only option, you are only using one-half of the healing power. I feel that when people incorporate these other healing modalities into the treatment of mental illness, they can live more blissful and purposeful lives.

If I could get Tommy back today, I would teach him more about spirituality rather than just how to hit a tennis ball with back spin or how to rollerblade backwards. We spent so much time doing physically oriented things, rather than spiritually oriented things, because I knew that's what he liked. I wish I would have pushed him out of his comfort zone and introduced him to the beautiful aspects of a spiritual life. I knew of those things, but I just concentrated on the things we had in common. Shouldn't spirituality be a necessary aspect of life, especially life with challenges like Tommy and Nick experienced? After all, Steve is living proof of the benefits of awakening to a life of spirituality.

I often think that the connection that I share with Steve is not only because he and I have a soul bond, but that Nick and my brother also have a soul bond. They were just so similar in life, had similar challenges, and they both left this Earth prematurely. I feel that they shared too many synchronicities for it not to be significant. And, from what psychics have told us, Tommy and Nick are connected on the other side. I truly feel that they are in The Place Between Here and There together and are either preparing to become spirit guides to assist those with imbalances or preparing to come back to Earth together and knock it out of the park next time. This gives me tremendous comfort.

When our loved ones pass over, can they see things that I don't want them to see?

It is true that we are always connected to those in spirit.

That connection is, however, limited to what is beneficial for your loved ones to know - like how you feel about something, the progress your soul is making in its incarnation, and the thoughts that you specifically send their way. They have no need to know the intimate details of your life, nor do they want to. Spirits do not need to possess any knowledge which does not help them evolve and grow or any knowledge which does not help their loved ones evolve and grow. So, do not worry about what they do and do not see.

Being that your loved ones are now in a place of love and light, they do not hold any grudges, animosities, or hard feelings. They now understand why everything in their life played out the way it did, and they are grateful for each moment, good or bad.

You and Kathie have such an incredible connection. Do you ever fight, or is it always paradise?

This is a great question, because people just assume that soulmates, twin flames, or spiritually connected people have wonderful relationships. They assume that these connections are effortless and easy. Nothing can be further from the truth. Being that everyone is a teacher, and everyone is a student, all interpersonal relationships have lessons within them. While Kathie and I do have a beautiful and loving relationship, we absolutely have the same challenges as other couples. We might even have more.

First, when couples embark on a spiritual path, they tend to expect more from each other. As our spirituality grows, we think that we are so evolved. However, if that is the case, I often wonder why we argue about whose turn it is to take out the trash.

Second, we are not above being critical of each other at times, although the language is somewhat different than that of most other couples we know. For example, when confronted with my short-tempered outbursts, Kathie often remarks "I am so excited to see that you have so much opportunity for personal growth."

Kathie and I share so many wonderful spiritual and physical excitements together, and I could not imagine my life without this beautiful, loving woman. I am very thankful for her patience, as I do have many opportunities for improvement.

Do you still ride a motorcycle?

The short answer is no, although I would if I could. I loved riding. It was such an important part of my life, for most of my life. I certainly am not afraid or apprehensive to ride. It is just what I love to do.

This recent motorcycle accident was not my first accident on the road. I had two previous accidents before this one, and countless accidents on my dirt bikes. It is just an accepted part of being a biker - you are going to have your "bell rung" every now and then. You have got to dust yourself off and get back up and ride. The difference now, however, is that my injuries were so severe from this accident that I had to have pins, rods and screws installed to put me back together. My body just could not handle another accident now. Even the smallest mishap could be life threatening.

Additionally, I had the opportunity to read all the Facebook posts from friends and loved ones expressing their deepest grief and their heartfelt wishes for my recovery. Even people who I thought did not like me at all said the kindest and most soulful things. My town even organized a food drive to bring me dinner every night for two months. In the end, knowing that people felt that way was the greatest gift that one can experience. I cannot state this emphatically enough to adequately express what I feel inside.

When I thought about the pain I caused everyone, I realized that this was not something I could, in good conscience, put them through again. Now that I knew that people actually cared about me, I had a joy in life that I had not had before. I have been given a wonderful gift of knowing how people felt about me, and I was not going to let them down.

As difficult as it was to give up my Harley, I found a new way to experience the thrill of riding, via the vehicle of a horse. As soon as I was able to walk again, I made a call to a small Western horseback riding ranch in eastern Long Island called Whispering Hooves. I had always been interested in horseback riding, and since I needed to replace one addiction with another, I thought this would be a safer one.

A wonderful and dedicated horsewoman named Katharine Barbarite ran the ranch. It was slow going at first, especially with all the hardware in my body, but this cowgirl was the best of the best and knew exactly how to work with my injuries. She was tough, and I appreciated that, as I did not want anyone babying me.

Riding her horses did wonders for my body, as I learned to move with the elegance of the horse's trots, lopes, and fast rides. Riding the trails with Katharine was just as exhilarating as riding the open road on my motorcycle. I even went on a week-long trip to Tombstone, Arizona, that Katharine hosts every year and did some serious riding.

Figure 38 - Steve at Whispering Hooves Ranch

Katharine moved her Whispering Hooves ranch out west, and I have not ridden since. However, when I retire and have more time on my hands, horseback riding is definitely going to return to my life. Riding a beautiful spirit animal like a horse is not only a physical experience, but a spiritual one as well.

Appendix 2:
Important Take-Aways

1) All situations in life have a dual meaning. One meaning is in the here and now. Another meaning is a spiritual meaning. When something negative occurs in your life, it can be an opportunity for intense soul growth. All experiences happen for a reason – all of them.

2) We cannot have animosity to anyone in life because all experiences are meant to teach us lessons that help our souls grow. In the end, some of our biggest agitators are our most important teachers, because their challenges force us to dig deep and find a way to succeed.

3) We must not judge others, because they are on their own spiritual path and will come to awareness in their own unique time. We are all at different levels of vibration. We might feel higher in vibration than others, but we have vibrated at every level ourselves, so living with patience, compassion, and love for others is essential for us, as well as it is for others.

4) Everyone and everything has a spirit – humans, animals, plants, stars, planets, and also what we perceive to be inanimate objects.

5) All of our spirits are connected and make up one, and that one is the Creator – the Creator and the creation are one. This is similar to the cells in the body. They all have their own consciousnesses, even though they are unaware of their connection, yet together they make up one body through their collective consciousness.

6) We have a higher self that remains in Heaven, while a portion of our soul comes to Earth for physical existence and learning. Our soul can be in many places at once. There is no one judging us. We are our own judge. We review our lives, and we feel the joys and pains we caused others. This is how we evolve and grow.

7) Everyone is a teacher and a student. Each experience we have with others is a lesson. Therefore, we must look for the lessons in all of our interactions with others, especially the most challenging interactions with the most challenging people (teachers).

8) Your most important teacher is yourself. We are solely responsible for our growth. Victim consciousness is a hindrance to soul growth.

9) A spirit is eternal, but it came from primordial creation. It was not born into its current state. It grows and develops from different incarnations and then it becomes, once again, part of the All That Is. As a result, the All That Is grows and evolves as well.

10) There is no central religion. We are all one. Religion is a means by which some can achieve their own enlightenment. All paths eventually lead to the destination of Christ-consciousness. When religions speak of God, they are actually all speaking of the same God consciousness, regardless of the dogma.

11) We can communicate with those who have crossed over or are in altered states of consciousness. Sometimes the communication is for our benefit, and sometimes the communication is for their benefit.

We always have help in life - from our higher self, spirit guides, departed loved ones, saints, angels, and ascended masters.

12) The Universe is always giving us signs that we are on a right or wrong path. Once we learn to read these signs, we will receive more.

13) Life is meant to be joyful. It is all a matter of perspective – how you look at life. You can use the same set of paints to paint a beautiful picture as you can to paint a sorrowful picture.

Appendix 3:
Journey into A Meditative Practice

The benefits of meditation are known the world over, and all the great masters were known to spend hours a day in meditation. This is not always possible for us due to time constraints, as we are very busy living in the modern world. Also, it is not easy for most people to go within and connect to their divine consciousnesses on their own.

Guided meditations are a wonderful start to a spiritual and meditative practice. I have been doing them for years, and I find them to be a perfect addiction, rather than other addictions that people use to calm their frazzled nerves and anxieties.

Biker Steve was not into meditation prior to his experience in The Place Between Here and There, but I happily taught him a thing or two about meditation. Now he is enjoying it immensely. Steve now meditates several times a day, even while walking on the beach. Between us, sometimes when he retires into the bedroom in the early evening and declares he is "going to meditate," his loud snoring causes me to think otherwise.

We wanted to include a simple and short 10-minute guided meditation to help you get started in a meditative practice. This meditation is a divine healing meditation that I created for our website, *www.BetweenHereAndThere.org*.

You can record this meditation and use it for yourself, your family, and your friends. We hope you enjoy it.

Divine Light Healing Meditation

I invite you to sit comfortably, in a chair or in a crossed-legged position, on the floor or on a yoga mat, or to lie down while doing this energy healing meditation.

Make any adjustments to ensure a comfortable position that you can maintain for ten minutes, because stillness is beneficial for going within and connecting to your divine inner spirit. If it is comfortable for you to do so, please close your eyes and focus on the third eye, located in between your brows. This is the seat of your intuition and helps you connect to your inner guidance system.

If you would like to use a mudra, which is a hand position that creates an energetic frequency, I Invite you to use one called Gyan Mudra, in which you place your hands on your knees or by your sides, palms facing up, with your thumbs and pointer fingers touching and the rest of your fingers straight. This opens you up to receiving divine wisdom.

We will begin by taking several deep cleansing breaths. Imagine that inside of your body, there is a pillar that runs from the bottoms of your feet all the way up to the crown of your head. When you take these cleansing breaths into your body, imagine a divine white light coming into the crown of your head, flushing out any negative thoughts, harmful memories, low-vibrating energetic frequencies, damaged cells, and whatever no longer serves your highest purpose. See these destructive impediments getting pushed down your pillar and out through your feet into Mother Earth. Mother Earth is a powerful living being that can transmute these negative energies into positive energies, which are then released back out to humanity for its highest good.

Continue taking these slow deep breaths, each one gently descending down your pillar and causing all the dark energetic forces to be eliminated and transmuted.

With each breath the divine white light within your pillar becomes more radiant as it overflows with the divine love from the magnificent Universe. See this healing energy magically returning your body to its divinity, as we are all beautiful spiritual beings of perfection having a human experience. As you continue to take in this cleansing and healing energy, you start to feel weightless and at one with your inner divine spirit.

Now that your body is in this divine state, while continuing to take long deep breaths, imagine that this higher state of consciousness allows you to travel across the ethers to a realm of even higher consciousness.

You find yourself sitting in a lush field of the greenest grass you have ever seen. There are majestic trees, in the most amazing shapes and sizes, sporadically situated in the field. Choose one to sit under. As you look around at this enchanting environment, you start to notice all the beautiful flowers – flowers that you have never seen before, in colors you have never seen before, and they emit the most glorious scents you have ever experienced. You begin to notice that there is a melodious sound that is coming from all around you. You realize that this sound is coming from everything around you. Everything in this ethereal place is actually vibrating with a mesmerizing frequency that creates music more tantalizing than anything you have ever heard.

As you are sitting under the tree, you also notice that everything is emitting love to you. Love is all around. You feel so uplifted and wonderful. You gaze into the distance, and you realize that you can see for what seems like miles and miles – stunning blue skies with shimmering white puffy clouds. Breathing long and deep, you sit for a while taking in all the grandeur.

As you settle into a peaceful calm, you notice dazzling flickering lights surrounding your periphery. These lights are spellbinding in their beauty, and they are slowly coming towards the field on which you sit. You begin to feel intoxicated by their loving energy, a feeling so deep and soul-enriching. As they get closer, you notice that they are all angels – the angels of Heaven – and they are surrounding the field, creating a protective ring around you now. You feel so much love, almost too much to bear. They do not speak, but you somehow understand that they want you to meet someone, and that someone is approaching you.

It is a magnificent being in a regal violet-colored robe. You can sense by its radiant appearance that this is a highly evolved soul. You feel so much love from this being as you look into its clear and wise eyes. You feel an immediate upgrading of your energy in the presence of this amazing being, and you also feel a familiarity, like you have been here before.

Suddenly, you realize something that takes you by utter surprise. This being is you. It is your higher self, the most ascended and perfect entity you have ever known. This is your higher self that remains in Heaven – as an ascended master – while a portion of you comes to Earth to learn and grow.

Your divine higher self places a hand on your shoulder and imparts new wisdom to you, letting you know that while you are having your human experience, he or she is always with you. You suddenly have the knowledge that with your positive thoughts, you have the ability to manifest perfect health, safety, success, confidence, courage, and love, and that all of your experiences on Earth have been grand and wonderful, as they have led you to this moment.

Your higher self could not be more proud of you. You need to forgive yourself and others for any negative experiences, because all that you have done has brought you to this one moment in time – the moment that you learn of your own power and divinity.

Your higher self lets you know that you always have a team of divine beings and angels surrounding you and looking to connect with you and guide you. You just have to call on them, through meditation or prayer. They will always give you the signs, synchronicities, and intuition you need to live your best life. In that moment, you feel all their love accelerating in a beautiful swirl of white protective light around your pillar. Your higher self tells you that this energetic protective barrier will remain with you as you return to your human experience. Nothing has ever felt more real and amazing to you.

Your higher self embraces you and lets you know that the time has come for you to return to Earth and be the divine beautiful spirit that you are, because the future of humanity's ascension into Heaven on Earth lies in everyone's remembrance of their divinity, and that you are a powerful creative being that will always retain healing and manifesting abilities – abilities that you can use not only for yourself and others, but for the planet as well. And, you can always call on your higher self and the angels whenever you desire. They will always be there for you.

Just then, you become weightless again and travel across the ethers, soaring like an eagle, and scanning the glorious Earth below. You feel powerful, because you are powerful. You land on your mat or chair and return to your physical body.

As you ground yourself back to this human existence, continue to take long, deep breaths. Your pillar is still filled with beautiful white light, but you notice that the light has now expanded all the way into your aura creating dazzling rays of shimmering light that, upon closer inspection, contain all the colors of the rainbow. You smile and realize that this is the gift promised by the angels. You did take it with you. You are divine, and all will be well because you now remember your divinity and the powerful being that you are.

Appendix 4:
Glossary

Akashic Records – the Akashic Records or hall of records is a multi-dimensional library in which all the information and wisdom pertaining to each soul ever incarnated is encoded. These records have existed since the beginning of time. It is believed that this information is the core part of the universal consciousness and can be compared to one's memory.

All That Is – the collective consciousness of all beings; the Source; the Universe; the Creator; God.

Angels – incorporeal beings, created by God at the dawn of time for the purpose of being his servants and messengers, who act as intermediaries between Heaven and humanity.

Angel number – sequential numbers that carry divine guidance by referring to special numerological meanings. In divine numerology, the science behind numbers, it is understood that each number carries with it a specific vibrational meaning that goes beyond a simple quantity. Angel numbers are, but are not limited to, 11, 111, 1111, 22, 222, 2222, 33, 333, 33333, etc.

Archangel – a powerful angel of the highest ranking in the angelic hierarchy who acts as a defender against evil in the world and a protector of incarnated souls. Michael, Gabriel, and Raphael are all archangels and are often misidentified as saints.

Asana – a body posture or pose - including reclining, standing, inverted, twisting and balancing poses – done during yoga or meditation practices.

Canonization – the act by which a Christian church declares that a person who has died is a saint, upon which declaration the person is included in the list of recognized saints, called the "canon."

Christ Consciousness – the state of mind in which one is in their highest divine alignment, radiating love and light, just like Jesus did while on Earth. It is the same consciousness of other spiritual masters, such as Buddha, Krishna, or Kuan Yin.

Continuation of Consciousness – the continuation of the soul after the demise of the physical body. Consciousness never dies; it is infinite. This consciousness is hosted in one's higher self or god spirit.

CPU – the central processing unit of a computer. Often referred in lay person's terms as the "main brain." The CPU is the primary component of a computer that processes instructions. In terms of computing power, the CPU is the most important element of a computer system.

Ego – the personality which is constructed within your reactive mind from your negative experiences. It is in constant conflict with your spiritual self and aggressively asserts itself when its existence is challenged when those negative behaviors are questioned.

Empty Nest Syndrome – the feeling that couples experience when their children leave home for college, marriage, or for a career. As so much of the parent's lives were focused on raising their children, a big void now exists requiring their lives to be re-evaluated and re-ordered.

Ethers – one of the Universe's five elements, which are ether, air, fire, water, and Earth. Ether is the most subtle of the five elements. Ether is the space in which the other elements fill. Ether is often associated with consciousness and has the properties of lightness, airiness, and spirituality.

Five Blue Ethers – the realms through which one travels after their physical bodies die on Earth until they merge with the creator. This can be thought of as the universal growth of the spirit's awareness through experiencing physical incarnations.

God Self – the totality of the soul, the higher self, the infinite spirit. That part of the spirit which links the physical incarnations with the continuation of consciousness.

ICU – an intensive care unit in a hospital which focuses on caring for patients with severe or life-threatening illnesses and injuries that require constant care, close supervision from life support equipment, and medication, in order to ensure that the patient is stabilized and is eventually transferred to a "step-down" unit.

Incarnation – one of a series of lifetimes that a person spends on Earth, or perhaps within another dimension or realm. This occurs when your infinite spirit takes on human form for the purpose of gaining experiences to fuel spiritual growth.

Infinite Spirit – the totality of the soul, the higher self. That part of oneself which was never born and will never die and is manifested in the continuation of consciousness. The infinite spirit's enlightenment evolves through each physical incarnation.

Kirtan – Sanskrit word that means reciting, narrating, telling, describing, i.e., an idea or story. In this case, it means the recitation of a chant through music in a concert-type setting, in which the audience sings along with the performers. Kirtan is often associated with a form of devotional yoga called Bhakti, which involves chanting names or mantras in devotion to the gods and goddesses.

Kriya – a series of postures (asanas), breath work (pranayama), and sound (mantra) that work toward a specific outcome in a yoga practice. Think of it as a prescription for better physical, mental, spiritual, and emotional health. For example, kriyas help to reduce stress, balance the negative mind, connect to the universal consciousness, or ground to mother Earth.

Kuan Yin (Quan Yin) – Chinese goddess of compassion, mercy and kindness. Often interpreted to be the divine feminine form of the spiritual Buddha. Due to her commitment to helping humans, she is approached with any concerns, troubles, or worries which people have in their everyday lives. The energy Kuan Yin expresses is best described as what a mother feels for her child. She is considered a Bodhisattva, which refers to a spiritual enlightenment just below that of the spiritual Buddha.

Kundalini Yoga – a practice of yoga in which the energy that lies dormant at the base of the spine becomes activated and channels upward through the chakras in the process of spiritual perfection. It is an uplifting blend of spiritual and physical practices incorporating movement, dynamic breathing, meditation, and chanting. The goal is to build physical vitality and increase spiritual consciousness.

Law of Attraction – the power of positive thinking to manifest what you desire in life. You are always in a state of creating your reality with every thought, either consciously or subconsciously. You will attract into your life whatever you focus on. If you stay focused on the positive things in your life, you will automatically attract more positive things into your life.

Mantra – a word or sound repeated to aid concentration in meditation. Chanting of mantras is an important part of the meditation process, enabling one to clear the "mind chatter" which often interferes with the meditation session.

Monkey Mind – state of mind in which one is very connected to simple or crude physical survival methods, without remorse or conscious feeling, rather than connected to enlightened actions with consequences and compassion.

Pran Sutra – a mantra that you can call upon and focus on at the time of your death for an easy transition into the next level of consciousness, or a mantra that you can use to help you stay blissful in life. Whenever your mind is fearful or has an unhealthy connection with the physical world, a Pran Sutra mantra will bring it back to a more grounded state. If you practice the same mantra regularly, it will penetrate your subconscious mind and will become part of your daily existence.

Prana – breath of vital energy of the body. In other traditions it is called chi, or qi, and could be thought of as those things that we take in and make a part of us. Unmanifested prana is the energy of pure consciousness and manifested prana is the force of creation, the original force of creation. When a person is well and balanced, prana flows unimpeded through the seven major chakra areas. However, when there are blockages or imbalances, physical, emotional, and spiritual issues are likely to occur.

Pranayama – practice of breath control in yoga. It consists of synchronizing the breath with the movements of the asanas (exercises) and is also a distinct breathing practice on its own. Pranayama serves as an important link between the outward, active practices of yoga, and the internal, surrendering practices that guide practitioners into deeper states of meditation and consciousness.

Purgatory – an intermediate and temporary state, according to some Christians, that exists after physical death, where one is punished or purified, in order to get ready to go on to Heaven.

RAM – random access memory on a computer. This is where information is stored for quick access by the computer's CPU. RAM doesn't remember everything forever. It is a "volatile" technology, meaning that once it loses power, it forgets everything forever.

Saint Germain – a legendary new age spiritual master, considered to be "The Lord of the Seventh Ray," who brings forth the violet flame, which transmutes spiritual negativity into positivity.

Saint Jude – one of the twelve apostles and a first cousin of Jesus. Saint Jude is the patron saint of desperate cases and lost causes. He is also often shown in icons with a flame around his head, which signifies the holy spirit, and holding an image of Jesus Christ, known as the Image of Edessa.

Saint Michael – Saint Michael is an archangel, rather than a saint. He is the leader of all the angels of the army of God. He is considered to be a champion of justice, the patron saint of police officers, a healer of the sick, and the guardian of the church.

Saint Therese – known as "the little flower of Jesus," Saint Therese was a Carmelite nun whose devotion and service to the order, as well as the myriad good deeds she accomplished in her short life of 24 years, resulted in her canonization. Saint Therese has been a highly influential mode of sanctity for others because of the simplicity and practicality of her approach to the spiritual life.

Six Million Dollar Man – a fictional television character from the 1970's, who was severely injured due to an accident. He was rebuilt by replacing several of his body parts with machinery, costing around six million dollars, making him very powerful and cyborg-like.

Spirit Guide – an entity that remains as a spirit to act as a guide or protector for a living incarnated human being. A person's spirit is raised to this level when entering the third blue ether. Spirit guides can be labeled as Archangels, Guardian Angels, Ascended Masters and Enlightened Beings, each capable of offering both comfort and sage advice during difficult times in your life.

The Secret – a best-selling book written by Rhonda Byrne in 2006, based on the belief of the law of attraction, which claims that thoughts can change a person's life directly.

Ten Bodies – Kundalini yoga philosophy that we have nine bodies other than the physical body. They are the soul body, which is literally our soul; the negative mind, which assesses our environment for danger and negative potential; the positive mind, which assesses our environment for what is beneficial, affirming, and positive; the neutral mind, which evaluates the assessments from the negative and positive minds to deliver guidance to us; the arc line, which gives us the ability to focus and meditate; the aura, which acts as a container for our life force energy and is a protective energetic shield; the pranic body, which is the breath that gives us life force; the subtle body, which holds our soul and carries us into the afterlife; and the radiant body, which is a field of energy that extends nine feet around us and sits on top of our aura.

Universal Consciousness – the single, intelligent unified consciousness that is comprised of all the consciousnesses of the beings that are in Heaven and in Earth. Yogis often refer to this consciousness as the Creator or God.

Ventilator – a ventilator is a mechanical system designed to pump air in and out of the lungs in order to deliver breaths to an individual who may not be able to breath on their own. The term ventilator and respirator are often used interchangeably by the lay person, although a respirator is specifically a protective face mask which filters air only.

Violet Flame – a miraculous invisible spiritual energy, the seventh ray of the Holy Spirit, that appears violet to those who have developed their spiritual vision. Invoking this ray into the body causes a transmutation of negative energy to positive energy, as well as love, mercy, justice and freedom.

Walls of Jericho – in the Bible, the walls of Jericho fell when Joshua's Israelite army marched around the city playing their trumpets.

Yahweh - the name of God in the ancient kingdoms of Israel and Judea. This name is not exclusive to Judaism or Christianity and has its roots in the pre-biblical spiritual customs of other cultures living in the land historically known as Canaan. The meaning of the name 'Yahweh' has been interpreted as "He Who Makes That Which Has Been Made" or "He Who Brings into Existence Whatever Exists."

Appendix 5:
Acknowledgements

This book was born out of the constant nudging of Kathie, some gentle and some not-so-much, but there were many others that heard about this story and urged us to tell it as well. They were the support system, because writing a book is not the easiest thing to do and when we became discouraged at the enormity of the task or experienced writer's block, their love and support were what kept us going.

Angela Blanchet, our dear friend, was the first person to hear our story and emphatically state that it was something that needed to be spoken about, written about, and shared. Having written two books herself, and self-published one of them, she provided guidance and encouragement regularly. Without her, we are sure that these pages would not have ever been printed, and we are forever grateful for her friendship, her assistance, and the light she shines in this world. She taught us positivity and the power of manifestation, and those are two things that were necessary for us to put this book together.

Theresa Banks, owner of Kundalini Yoga of Long Island, became our good friend after attending yoga classes at her studio. After hearing our story and suggesting that it needed to be shared with the public, she was extremely generous in providing free use of her studio for our first The Place Between Here and There workshop. She also ensured the entire yoga community came to the event, which led to rave reviews and successive workshops. Theresa was instrumental in the success of our journey, and we are forever grateful.

Anita Weber, my beautiful and amazing mother, was the first recipient and our biggest fan of the book. Her continuous encouragement was the steam that kept our ship going. Her faith in us, her love for us, and her endless positivity was what sustained us every day of the process.

Tom Hayes, Kathie's dad, is one of the most remarkable men I have ever met. His assistance in every aspect of our lives, including being our consistent sounding board, was instrumental in the completion of this book. We cannot thank him enough for all he does for us, and for everyone, because he's just that kind of guy.

Figure 39 - Siblings Steve, Scott, Darlene and Sherri

Scott Weber, my brother, along with his family, were the reason I made it through the arduous recovery process after the accident. Their love, companionship, and dedication meant everything to me. Without them, I could never have done this.

Darlene Sutherland, my sister, my angel, who looked after me during the most critical early days in the hospital. She was a guiding voice to both the medical staff and our family.

If it was not for her love and compassion, it is likely that I would not have survived to share this experience.

Sherri Dunne, my sister, who would visit me each day when I was in the coma and sing to me as she did when I was a young child. That voice was so comforting to me and helped guide me back through the ethers to all the people who I loved and who loved me.

Angel Weber, my beautiful daughter, will forever be my inspiration for loving, for living, and for making the world a better place. Her love and light are the reason my heart beats. I am eternally grateful for her and will always strive to be the best me that I can be to make her proud. She is the reason I am successful at anything in life.

Kristen Plant, Kathie's daughter and a beautiful, compassionate soul, who was with us during every part of this process. Her radiant spirituality, as well as her old soul level of awareness, provided much-needed advice and support for all of the experiences detailed in this book. Kathie always says, "When I grow up, I want to be just like Kristen," and that is a testament to the wonderful woman Kristen is.

Sean Reilly, Kristen's boyfriend, aspiring hockey player, musician, songwriter, and Place Between Here and There workshop singer. He is a light worker that was placed into our lives from the Heavens.

Lisa Titone, my cousin and our best friend, was a crucial part of our amazing journey. She is a sister to both Kathie and me. The Universe chose her to bring this most important message to us. And once again, the Universe chose wisely. We could not have completed this book without her love and support.

Lee Knight, a multi-talented musician, author, dancer and yoga teacher. Lee shared her beautiful music at every one of our workshops. Her positivity and exuberance were a key to our success. She is surely a beacon of love and light.

Cristen Blundell, Kathie's dear friend, and biggest fan of ours, who attended every workshop and assisted with the videotaping process. She was a necessary grounding force for Kathie, who had a fear of speaking in public. We are so grateful for Cristen's love and support.

Larry Noon, my buddy, has been at my side during all my motorcycle riding years, then at my side during all my days in the hospital as well. He and I shared the road, side by side during the good times as well as the not-so-good times. It came to no surprise to me to find him at my side when I was in my hospital bed. I am so grateful for all that he has done for me in this lifetime.

The doctors, nurses and staff at Stony Brook University Hospital are the reason I am alive today. Without them, this book could not have been written. I am forever grateful for their expertise in saving human lives.

The community of yoga friends that we have is so critical to our lives and to this book. We could not have been the sane and soulful beings that we are without them; and, therefore, could not have completed this project without their love, their light, and their support. It is impossible to name them all, but they are the entire communities of Kundalini Yoga of Long Island in Northport, and Family Tree Yoga in Nesconset.

Gerry LoDuca and my coworkers at DUKAL Corporation, who supported me during the most challenging times of my life. All of these bright souls bring both love and spirit into their work, and, dare I say, play as well.

Peace and Love Always

Stephen and Katherine

If you would like to stay connected with us, please join us at:

Email: info@BetweenHereAndThere.org
Facebook: www.betweenhereandthere.org
YouTube: www.theplacebetweenhereandthere.com

Communicate with the authors - Share your comments and hear what others are saying - Ask questions - Find out about upcoming workshops - Book workshops for your venue -Learn about future book projects

Made in the USA
Middletown, DE
25 August 2024